Gospel Principles

Published by
The Church of Jesus Christ of Latter-day Saints
Salt Lake City, Utah

Your comments and suggestions about this book would be appreciated. Please submit them to Curriculum Development, 50 East North Temple Street, Salt Lake City, Utah 84150-0024. E-mail: cur-development@ldschurch.org. Please list your name, address, ward, and stake. Be sure to give the title of the book. Then offer your comments and suggestions about the book's strengths and areas of potential improvement.

Printed in the United States of America

English approval: 5/07

To Lie Is Dishonest

Lying is intentionally deceiving others. Bearing false witness is one form of lying. The Lord gave this commandment to the children of Israel: "Thou shalt not bear false witness against thy neighbour" (Exodus 20:16). Jesus also taught this when He was on earth (see Matthew 19:18). There are many other forms of lying. When we speak untruths, we are guilty of lying. We can also intentionally deceive others by a gesture or a look, by silence, or by telling only part of the truth. Whenever we lead people in any way to believe something that is not true, we are not being honest.

The Lord is not pleased with such dishonesty, and we will have to account for our lies. Satan would have us believe it is all right to lie. He says, "Yea, lie a little; . . . there is no harm in this" (2 Nephi 28:8). Satan encourages us to justify our lies to ourselves. Honest people will recognize Satan's temptations and will speak the whole truth, even if it seems to be to their disadvantage.

To Steal Is Dishonest

Jesus taught, "Thou shalt not steal" (Matthew 19:18). Stealing is taking something that does not belong to us. When we take what belongs to someone else or to a store or to the community without permission, we are stealing. Taking merchandise or supplies from an employer is stealing. Copying music, movies, pictures, or written text without the permission of the copyright owners is dishonest and is a form of theft. Accepting more change or goods than one should is dishonest. Taking more than our share of anything is stealing.

To Cheat Is Dishonest

We cheat when we give less than we owe, or when we get something we do not deserve. Some employees cheat their employers by not working their full time; yet they accept full pay. Some employers

---

For teachers: This chapter contains three sections that describe forms of dishonesty: lying, stealing, and cheating. You might consider dividing class members or family members into three groups. Assign each group one of these three sections. Ask the individuals in each group to silently read their assigned section and consider the forms of dishonesty described in that section. Then discuss the sections as a class or as a family. Ask how we can be honest in each of the situations described.

are not fair to their employees; they pay them less than they should. Satan says, "Take the advantage of one because of his words, dig a pit for thy neighbor" (2 Nephi 28:8). Taking unfair advantage is a form of dishonesty. Providing inferior service or merchandise is cheating.

We Must Not Excuse Our Dishonesty

• What happens to us spiritually when we excuse our dishonesty?

People use many excuses for being dishonest. People lie to protect themselves and to have others think well of them. Some excuse themselves for stealing, thinking they deserve what they took, intend to return it, or need it more than the owner. Some cheat to get better grades in school or because "everyone else does it" or to get even.

These excuses and many more are given as reasons for dishonesty. To the Lord, there are no acceptable reasons. When we excuse ourselves, we cheat ourselves and the Spirit of God ceases to be with us. We become more and more unrighteous.

We Can Be Completely Honest

• What does it mean to be completely honest?

To become completely honest, we must look carefully at our lives. If there are ways in which we are being even the least bit dishonest, we should repent of them immediately.

When we are completely honest, we cannot be corrupted. We are true to every trust, duty, agreement, or covenant, even if it costs us money, friends, or our lives. Then we can face the Lord, ourselves, and others without shame. President Joseph F. Smith counseled, "Let every man's life be so that his character will bear the closest inspection, and that it may be seen as an open book, so that he will have nothing to shrink from or be ashamed of" (*Gospel Doctrine,* 5th ed. [1939], 252).

• In what ways does our honesty or dishonesty affect how we feel about ourselves?

Additional Scriptures

- D&C 50:17 (speak only by the spirit of truth)
- D&C 76:103–6 (destination of liars)
- D&C 42:27 (commandment not to speak evil of neighbors)
- Exodus 20:15–16 (commandments not to steal and not to bear false witness)
- D&C 42:20, 84–85; 59:6 (forbidden to steal)
- D&C 3:2 (God is honest)
- D&C 10:25–28 (Satan deceives)

Tithes and Offerings

Chapter 32

Paying Tithes and Offerings

- How does our willingness to pay tithes and offerings show gratitude to our Heavenly Father for all His blessings to us?

We have been given commandments to help us prepare in every way to live in the presence of our Heavenly Father. He has given us a way to thank Him for our blessings. Willingly paying tithes and offerings is one way we thank Him. As we pay these offerings, we show that we love Him and will obey His counsel.

- In what ways does the payment of tithes and offerings help us thank our Heavenly Father?

Obeying the Law of Tithing

- What is an honest tithe?

Anciently, Abraham and Jacob obeyed the commandment to pay a tithe of one-tenth of their increase (see Hebrews 7:1–10; Genesis 14:19–20; 28:20–22).

In modern times the Prophet Joseph Smith prayed, "O Lord, show unto thy servants how much thou requirest of the properties of thy people for a tithing" (D&C 119, section introduction). The Lord answered: "This shall be the beginning of the tithing of my people. And after that, those who have thus been tithed shall pay one-tenth of all their interest annually; and this shall be a standing law unto them forever" (D&C 119:3–4). The First Presidency has explained that "one-tenth of all their interest annually" refers to our income (see First Presidency letter, Mar. 19, 1970).

For teachers: Use questions at the beginning of a section to start a discussion and send class members or family members to the text to find more information. Use questions at the end of a section to help class members or family members ponder and discuss the meaning of what they have read and apply it in their lives.

When we pay tithing we show our faithfulness to the Lord. We also teach our children the value of this law. They will want to follow our example and pay tithing on any money they receive.

- In what ways is tithing a principle of faith more than a principle of finances?
- What can parents do to teach their children to pay tithing and understand its importance?

We Should Give Willingly

- Why is our attitude important as we pay tithing?

It is important to give willingly. "When one pays his tithing without enjoyment he is robbed of a part of the blessing. He must learn to give cheerfully, willingly and joyfully, and his gift will be blessed" (Stephen L Richards, *The Law of Tithing* [pamphlet, 1983], 8).

The Apostle Paul taught that how we give is as important as what we give. He said, "Let him give; not grudgingly, or of necessity: for God loveth a cheerful giver" (2 Corinthians 9:7).

- What does it mean to you to be a "cheerful giver"?

Tithing and Other Offerings

- In what ways does the Church use tithing funds and other offerings?

As members of the Church, we give tithing and other offerings to the Lord.

Tithing

Tithing is used by the Church for many purposes. Some of these are to:

1. Build, maintain, and operate temples, meetinghouses, and other buildings.
2. Provide operating funds for stakes, wards, and other units of the Church. (These units use the funds to carry out the ecclesiastical programs of the Church, which include teaching the gospel and conducting social activities.)

3. Help the missionary program.
4. Educate young people in Church schools, seminaries, and institutes.
5. Print and distribute lesson materials.
6. Help in family history and temple work.

Other Offerings

Fast Offerings. Church members fast each month by going without food and drink for two consecutive meals. They contribute at least the amount of money they would have spent for the meals. They may give as generously as they are able. This offering is called the fast offering. Bishops use these fast offerings to provide food, shelter, clothing, and medical care for the needy. (See chapter 25 in this book.)

As part of the fast day, members attend a meeting called the fast and testimony meeting, where they share with each other their testimonies of Christ and His gospel.

Other Donations. Church members may donate to other efforts of the Church, such as missionary work, the Perpetual Education Fund, temple construction, and humanitarian aid.

Service. Members also offer their time, skills, and goods to help others. This service allows the Church to help needy members and nonmembers around the world at community, national, and international levels, especially when disasters occur.

We Are Blessed When We Give Tithes and Offerings

The Lord promises to bless us as we faithfully pay our tithes and offerings. He said, "Bring ye all the tithes into the storehouse, that there may be meat in mine house, and prove me now herewith . . . if I will not open you the windows of heaven, and pour you out a blessing, that there shall not be room enough to receive it" (Malachi 3:10).

Latter-day revelation tells of another blessing for those who tithe: "Verily it is a day of sacrifice, and a day for the tithing of my people; for he that is tithed shall not be burned at his coming" (D&C 64:23).

The blessings we have been promised are both material and spiritual. If we give willingly, Heavenly Father will help us provide for our daily needs of food, clothes, and shelter. Speaking to Latter-day Saints in the Philippines, President Gordon B. Hinckley said that if people "will accept the gospel and live it, pay their tithes and offerings, even though those be meager, the Lord will keep His ancient promise in their behalf, and they will have rice in their bowls and clothing on their backs and shelter over their heads. I do not see any other solution. They need a power greater than any earthly power to lift them and help them" ("Inspirational Thoughts," *Ensign,* Aug. 1997, 7). The Lord will also help us grow "in a knowledge of God, and in a testimony, and in the power to live the gospel and to inspire our families to do the same" (*Teachings of Presidents of the Church: Heber J. Grant* [2002], 124).

Those who pay their tithes and offerings are greatly blessed. They have a good feeling that they are helping to build the kingdom of God on earth.

- What are some blessings you, your family members, or your friends have received through the payment of tithing and other offerings?

Additional Scriptures

- D&C 119:1–4 (the law of tithing)
- Genesis 14:18–20; Alma 13:13–16 (Abraham paid tithes)

Missionary Work

Chapter 33

The Lord's Church Is a Missionary Church

• In what ways is missionary work part of God's plan for His children?

The Lord revealed the gospel plan to Adam: "And thus the Gospel began to be preached, from the beginning" (Moses 5:58). Later, Adam's righteous descendants were sent to preach the gospel: "They . . . called upon all men, everywhere, to repent; and faith was taught unto the children of men" (Moses 6:23).

All the prophets have been missionaries. Each in his day was commanded to preach the gospel message. Whenever the priesthood has been on the earth, the Lord has needed missionaries to preach the eternal principles of the gospel to His children.

The Lord's Church has always been a missionary church. When the Savior lived on the earth, He ordained Apostles and Seventies and gave them the authority and responsibility to preach the gospel. Most of their preaching was to their own people, the Jews (see Matthew 10:5–6). After Jesus was resurrected, He sent Apostles to preach the gospel to the Gentiles. He commanded the Apostles, "Go ye into all the world, and preach the gospel to every creature" (Mark 16:15).

The Apostle Paul was a great missionary sent to the Gentiles. After he was converted to the Church, he spent the remainder of his life preaching the gospel to them. At different times during his mission he was whipped, stoned, and imprisoned. Yet he continued to preach the gospel (see Acts 23:10–12; 26).

Missionary work began again when the Lord's Church was restored through the Prophet Joseph Smith. Today the Apostles

For teachers: Sharing experiences with gospel principles can invite the Spirit. You may want to contact a few class members or family members in advance, asking them to prepare to share experiences that are meaningful to them and that may help others.

and Seventies have been given the chief responsibility for preaching the gospel and seeing that it is preached in all the world. The Lord told Joseph Smith: "Proclaim my gospel from land to land, and from city to city. . . . Bear testimony in every place, unto every people" (D&C 66:5, 7). In June 1830, Samuel Harrison Smith, the Prophet's brother, began the first missionary journey for the Church.

Since that time, over one million missionaries have been called and sent forth to preach the gospel. The message they take to the world is that Jesus Christ is the Son of God and our Savior. They testify that the gospel has been restored to the earth through a prophet of God. The missionaries are given the responsibility to preach the gospel to all people, to baptize them, and to teach them to do all things that the Lord has commanded (see Matthew 28:19–20). Latter-day Saint missionaries go at their own expense to all parts of the world to preach the gospel message.

The Gospel Will Be Preached to All the World

- What are some different ways the Lord has prepared for us to share the gospel?

We have been told in latter-day revelation that we must take the restored gospel to every nation and people (see D&C 133:37). The Lord never gives us a commandment without preparing a way for us to accomplish it (see 1 Nephi 3:7). The Lord has prepared ways for us to teach the gospel in nations that were once closed to us. As we continue to pray and exercise faith, the Lord will open other nations to missionary work.

The Lord is also "inspiring the minds of great people to create inventions that further the work of the Lord in ways this world has never known" (Russell M. Nelson, in "Computerized Scriptures Now Available," *Ensign,* Apr. 1988, 73). Newspapers, magazines, television, radio, satellites, computers, the Internet, and related technology help give the gospel message to millions of people. We who have the fulness of the gospel need to use these inventions to fulfill the Lord's commandment: "For, verily, the sound must go forth from this place into all the world, and unto the uttermost parts of the earth—the gospel must be preached unto every [person]" (D&C 58:64).

- In what ways have you seen technology used effectively to share the gospel?

Missionary Work Is Important

- Why is it important for each person to hear and understand the gospel?

"This is our first interest as a Church—to save and exalt the souls of the children of men" (Ezra Taft Benson, in Conference Report, Apr. 1974, 151; or *Ensign,* May 1974, 104). Missionary work is necessary in order to give the people of the world an opportunity to hear and accept the gospel. They need to learn the truth, turn to God, and receive forgiveness from their sins.

Many of our brothers and sisters on earth are blinded by false teachings and "are only kept from the truth because they know not where to find it" (D&C 123:12). Through missionary work we can bring them the truth.

The Lord has commanded, "Labor ye in my vineyard for the last time—for the last time call upon the inhabitants of the earth" (D&C 43:28). As we teach the gospel to our brothers and sisters, we are preparing the way for the Second Coming of the Savior (see D&C 34:6).

We Should All Be Missionaries

- In what ways can we actively seek opportunities to share the gospel with others? In what ways can we prepare ourselves for such opportunities?

Every member of the Church is a missionary. We should be missionaries even if we are not formally called and set apart. We are responsible to teach the gospel by word and deed to all of our Heavenly Father's children. The Lord has told us, "It becometh every man who hath been warned to warn his neighbor" (D&C 88:81). We have been told by a prophet that we should show our neighbors that we love them before we warn them (see *Teachings of Presidents of the Church: Spencer W. Kimball* [2006], 262). They need to experience our friendship and fellowship.

The sons of Mosiah willingly accepted their responsibility to teach the gospel. When they were converted to the Church, their hearts were filled with compassion for others. They wanted to preach the gospel to their enemies the Lamanites, "for they could not bear that any human soul should perish; yea, even the very thoughts that any soul should endure endless torment did cause them to quake and tremble" (Mosiah 28:3). As the gospel fills our lives with joy, we will feel this kind of love and compassion for our brothers and sisters. We will want to share the message of the gospel with everyone who desires to listen.

There are many ways we can share the gospel. Following are some suggestions:

1. We can show friends and others the joy we experience from living the truths of the gospel. In this way we will be a light to the world (see Matthew 5:16).
2. We can overcome our natural shyness by being friendly to others and doing kind things for them. We can help them see that we are sincerely interested in them and are not seeking personal gain.
3. We can explain the gospel to nonmember friends and others.
4. We can invite friends who are interested in learning more about the gospel into our homes to be taught by the missionaries. If our nonmember friends live too far away, we can request that missionaries in their areas visit them.
5. We can teach our children the importance of sharing the gospel, and we can prepare them spiritually and financially to go on missions. We can also prepare ourselves to serve full-time missions in our senior years.
6. We can pay our tithing and contribute to the missionary fund. These donations are used for furthering missionary work.
7. We can contribute to the ward, branch, or general missionary fund to give financial support to missionaries whose families are unable to support them.

8. We can do family history research and temple work to help our ancestors receive the full blessings of the gospel.
9. We can invite nonmembers to activities such as family home evenings and Church socials, conferences, and meetings.
10. We can give copies of Church magazines. We can also share gospel messages by using features available on the Church's official Internet sites, LDS.org and Mormon.org.

Our Heavenly Father will help us be effective missionaries when we have the desire to share the gospel and pray for guidance. He will help us find ways to share the gospel with those around us.

- Think about people you can share the gospel with. Decide how you will do so. Consider setting a goal to share the gospel with these people by a certain date.

The Lord Promises Us Blessings for Doing Missionary Work

The Lord told the Prophet Joseph Smith that missionaries would receive great blessings. Speaking to elders who were returning from their missions, the Lord said, "Ye are blessed, for the testimony which ye have borne is recorded in heaven for the angels to look upon; and they rejoice over you" (D&C 62:3). He has also said that those who work for the salvation of others will have their sins forgiven and will bring salvation to their own souls (see D&C 4:4; 31:5; 84:61).

The Lord has told us:

"If it so be that you should labor all your days in crying repentance unto this people, and bring, save it be one soul unto me, how great shall be your joy with him in the kingdom of my Father!

"And now, if your joy will be great with one soul that you have brought unto me into the kingdom of my Father, how great will be your joy if you should bring many souls unto me!" (D&C 18:15–16).

- When have you experienced the joy of missionary work?

Additional Scriptures

- D&C 1:17–23 (Joseph Smith commanded to preach)
- D&C 24:12 (Lord strengthens those who always seek to declare His gospel)
- D&C 38:41 (share the gospel in mildness and meekness)
- D&C 34:4–6; Acts 5:42 (gospel to be preached)
- D&C 60:1–2 (Lord warns those who are afraid to preach the gospel)
- D&C 75:2–5 (those who declare the gospel and are faithful will be blessed with eternal life)
- D&C 88:81–82 (all those who have been warned should warn their neighbors)
- Matthew 24:14 (gospel to be preached before the end shall come)
- Abraham 2:9–11 (gospel and priesthood to be given to all nations)

Developing Our Talents

Chapter 34

We All Have Different Talents and Abilities

We all have special gifts, talents, and abilities given to us by our Heavenly Father. When we were born, we brought these gifts, talents, and abilities with us (see chapter 2 in this book).

The prophet Moses was a great leader, but he needed Aaron, his brother, to help as a spokesman (see Exodus 4:14–16). Some of us are leaders like Moses or good speakers like Aaron. Some of us can sing well or play an instrument. Others of us may be good in sports or able to work well with our hands. Other talents we might have are understanding others, patience, cheerfulness, or the ability to teach others.

- How have you benefited from the talents of others?

We Should Use and Improve Our Talents

- How can we develop our talents?

We have a responsibility to develop the talents we have been given. Sometimes we think we do not have many talents or that other people have been blessed with more abilities than we possess. Sometimes we do not use our talents because we are afraid that we might fail or be criticized by others. We should not hide our talents. We should use them. Then others can see our good works and glorify our Heavenly Father (see Matthew 5:16).

There are certain things we must do to develop our talents. First, we must discover our talents. We should evaluate ourselves to find our strengths and abilities. Our family and friends can help us do this.

For teachers: One way to show class members that you care about them individually is to call them by name. Learn their names. When new class members attend the class, introduce them to the others.

We should also ask our Heavenly Father to help us learn about our talents.

Second, we must be willing to spend the time and effort to develop the talent we are seeking.

Third, we must have faith that our Heavenly Father will help us, and we must have faith in ourselves.

Fourth, we must learn the skills necessary for us to develop our talents. We might do this by taking a class, asking a friend to teach us, or reading a book.

Fifth, we must practice using our talent. Every talent takes effort and work to develop. The mastery of a talent must be earned.

Sixth, we must share our talent with others. It is by our using our talents that they grow (see Matthew 25:29).

All of these steps are easier if we pray and seek the Lord's help. He wants us to develop our talents, and He will help us.

We Can Develop Our Talents in Spite of Our Weaknesses

- How can we develop our talents in spite of our weaknesses?

Because we are mortal and fallen, we have weaknesses. With the Lord's help, our weakness and fallen nature can be overcome (see Ether 12:27, 37). Beethoven composed his greatest music after he was deaf. Enoch overcame his slowness of speech to become a powerful teacher (see Moses 6:26–47).

Some great athletes have had to overcome handicaps before they have succeeded in developing their talents. Shelly Mann was such an example. "At the age of five she had polio. . . . Her parents took her daily to a swimming pool where they hoped the water would help hold her arms up as she tried to use them again. When she could lift her arm out of the water with her own power, she cried for joy. Then her goal was to swim the width of the pool, then the length, then several lengths. She kept on trying, swimming, enduring, day after day after day, until she won the [Olympic] gold medal for the butterfly stroke—one of the most difficult of all swimming strokes" (Marvin J. Ashton, in Conference Report, Apr. 1975, 127; or *Ensign,* May 1975, 86).

Heber J. Grant overcame many of his weaknesses and turned them into talents. He had as a motto these words: "That which we persist in doing becomes easier for us to do; not that the nature of the thing is changed, but that our power to do is increased" (in *Teachings of Presidents of the Church: Heber J. Grant* [2002], 35).

The Lord Will Bless Us If We Use Our Talents Wisely

President Joseph F. Smith said, "Every son and every daughter of God has received some talent, and each will be held to strict account for the use or misuse to which it is put" (*Gospel Doctrine,* 5th ed. [1939], 370). A talent is one kind of stewardship (responsibility in the kingdom of God). The parable of the talents tells us that when we serve well in our stewardship, we will be given greater responsibilities. If we do not serve well, our stewardship will eventually be taken from us. (See Matthew 25:14–30.)

We are also told in the scriptures that we will be judged according to our works (see Matthew 16:27). By developing and using our talents for other people, we perform good works.

The Lord is pleased when we use our talents wisely. He will bless us if we use our talents to benefit other people and to build up His kingdom here on earth. Some of the blessings we gain are joy and love from serving our brothers and sisters here on earth. We also learn self-control. All these things are necessary if we are going to be worthy to live with our Heavenly Father again.

- What are some examples of people whose talents have been magnified because they used them wisely? (Consider people you know or people in the scriptures or Church history.)

Additional Scriptures

- James 1:17 (gifts come from God)
- D&C 46:8–11; 1 Timothy 4:14 (seek and develop gifts)
- 2 Corinthians 12:9 (weak things made strong)
- Revelation 20:13; 1 Nephi 15:33; D&C 19:3 (judged by our works)
- Hebrews 13:21 (show good works)

Obedience

Chapter 35

We Should Obey God Willingly

- What difference does it make to obey willingly rather than unwillingly?

When Jesus was on the earth, a lawyer asked Him a question:

"Master, which is the great commandment in the law?

"Jesus said unto him, Thou shalt love the Lord thy God with all thy heart, and with all thy soul, and with all thy mind.

"This is the first and great commandment.

"And the second is like unto it, Thou shalt love thy neighbour as thyself.

"On these two commandments hang all the law and the prophets" (Matthew 22:36–40).

From these scriptures we learn how important it is for us to love the Lord and our neighbors. But how do we show our love for the Lord?

Jesus answered this question when He said, "He that hath my commandments, and keepeth them, he it is that loveth me: and he that loveth me shall be loved of my Father" (John 14:21).

Each of us should ask ourselves why we obey God's commandments. Is it because we fear punishment? Is it because we desire the rewards for living a good life? Is it because we love God and Jesus Christ and want to serve Them?

It is better to obey the commandments because we fear punishment than not to obey them at all. But we will be much happier if we obey God because we love Him and want to obey Him. When

For teachers: You can help class members or family members think more deeply about a question by giving them time to ponder. After they have had enough time, ask for their responses.

we obey Him freely, He can bless us freely. He said, "I, the Lord, . . . delight to honor those who serve me in righteousness and in truth unto the end" (D&C 76:5). Obedience also helps us progress and become more like our Heavenly Father. But those who do nothing until they are commanded and then keep the commandments unwillingly lose their reward (see D&C 58:26–29).

- How can we increase our desire to obey?

We Can Obey without Understanding Why

- Why do we not always need to understand the Lord's purposes in order to be obedient?

By keeping God's commandments, we prepare for eternal life and exaltation. Sometimes we do not know the reason for a particular commandment. However, we show our faith and trust in God when we obey Him without knowing why.

Adam and Eve were commanded to offer sacrifices to God. One day an angel appeared to Adam and asked why he offered sacrifices. Adam replied that he did not know the reason. He did it because the Lord commanded him. (See Moses 5:5–6 and the picture in this chapter.)

The angel then taught Adam the gospel and told him of the Savior who was to come. The Holy Ghost fell upon Adam, and Adam prophesied concerning the inhabitants of the earth down to the last generation. (See Moses 5:7–10; D&C 107:56.) This knowledge and great blessings came to Adam because he was obedient.

God Will Prepare a Way

The Book of Mormon tells us that Nephi and his older brothers received a very difficult assignment from the Lord (see 1 Nephi 3:1–6). Nephi's brothers complained, saying that the Lord required a hard thing of them. But Nephi said, "I will go and do the things which the Lord hath commanded, for I know that the Lord giveth no commandments unto the children of men, save he shall prepare a way for them that they may accomplish the thing which he commandeth them" (1 Nephi 3:7). When we find it difficult to obey a commandment of the Lord, we should remember Nephi's words.

- When has the Lord prepared a way for you to obey Him?

No Commandment Is Too Small or Too Great to Obey

Sometimes we may think a commandment is not very important. The scriptures tell of a man named Naaman who thought that way. Naaman had a dreadful disease and traveled from Syria to Israel to ask the prophet Elisha to heal him. Naaman was an important man in his own country, so he was offended when Elisha did not greet him in person but sent his servant instead. Naaman was even more offended when he received Elisha's message: wash seven times in the river Jordan. "Are not [the] rivers of Damascus better than all the waters of Israel? may I not wash in them, and be clean?" he demanded. He went away in a rage. But his servants asked him: "If the prophet had bid thee do some great thing, wouldest thou not have done it? how much rather then, when he saith to thee, Wash, and be clean?" Naaman was wise enough to understand that it was important to obey the prophet of God, even if it seemed a small matter. So he washed in the Jordan and was healed. (See 2 Kings 5:1–14.)

Sometimes we may think a commandment is too difficult for us to obey. Like Nephi's brothers, we may say, "It is a hard thing God requires of us." Yet, like Nephi, we can be sure that God will give us no commandment unless He prepares a way for us to obey Him.

It was a "hard thing" when the Lord commanded Abraham to offer his beloved son Isaac as a sacrifice (see Genesis 22:1–13; see also chapter 26 in this book). Abraham had waited many years for the birth of Isaac, the son God had promised him. How could he lose his son in such a way? This commandment must have been exceedingly difficult for Abraham. Yet he chose to obey God.

We too should be willing to do anything God requires. The Prophet Joseph Smith said, "I made this my rule: *When the Lord commands, do it*" (*Teachings of Presidents of the Church: Joseph Smith* [2007], 160). This can be our rule also.

- When have you received blessings as a result of your obedience to commandments that seemed small?

Jesus Christ Obeyed His Father

- What examples come to mind when you think of Jesus Christ obeying His Father?

Jesus Christ was the sublime example of obedience to our Heavenly Father. He said, "I came down from heaven, not to do mine own will, but the will of him that sent me" (John 6:38). His whole life was devoted to obeying His Father; yet it was not always easy for him. He was tempted in all ways as other mortals (see Hebrews 4:15). In the Garden of Gethsemane He prayed, saying, "O my Father, if it be possible, let this cup pass from me: nevertheless not as I will, but as thou wilt" (Matthew 26:39).

Because Jesus obeyed the Father's will in all things, He made salvation possible for all of us.

- How can remembering the Savior's example help us be obedient?

Results of Obedience and Disobedience

- What are the consequences of obeying or disobeying the Lord's commandments?

The kingdom of heaven is governed by law, and when we receive any blessing, it is by obedience to the law upon which that blessing is based (see D&C 130:20–21; 132:5). The Lord has told us that through our obedience and diligence we may gain knowledge and intelligence (see D&C 130:18–19). We may also grow spiritually (see Jeremiah 7:23–24). On the other hand, disobedience brings disappointment and results in a loss of blessings. "Who am I, saith the Lord, that have promised and have not fulfilled? I command and men obey not; I revoke and they receive not the blessing. Then they say in their hearts: This is not the work of the Lord, for his promises are not fulfilled" (D&C 58:31–33).

When we keep the commandments of God, He fulfills His promises, as King Benjamin told his people: "He doth require that ye should do as he hath commanded you; for which if ye do, he doth immediately bless you" (Mosiah 2:24).

The Obedient Gain Eternal Life

The Lord counsels us, "If you keep my commandments and endure to the end you shall have eternal life, which gift is the greatest of all the gifts of God" (D&C 14:7).

The Lord has described other blessings that will come to those who obey Him in righteousness and truth until the end:

"Thus saith the Lord—I, the Lord, am merciful and gracious unto those who fear me, and delight to honor those who serve me in righteousness and in truth unto the end.

"Great shall be their reward and eternal shall be their glory.

"And to them will I reveal all mysteries, yea, all the hidden mysteries of my kingdom from days of old, and for ages to come, will I make known unto them the good pleasure of my will concerning all things pertaining to my kingdom.

"Yea, even the wonders of eternity shall they know, and things to come will I show them, even the things of many generations.

"And their wisdom shall be great, and their understanding reach to heaven. . . .

"For by my Spirit will I enlighten them, and by my power will I make known unto them the secrets of my will—yea, even those things which eye has not seen, nor ear heard, nor yet entered into the heart of man" (D&C 76:5–10).

- What does the phrase "endure to the end" mean to you?
- What can we do to stay true to gospel principles even when it is unpopular to do so? How can we help children and youth stay true to gospel principles?

Additional Scriptures

- Abraham 3:25 (we came to earth to prove our obedience)
- 1 Samuel 15:22 (obedience is better than sacrifice)

- Ecclesiastes 12:13; John 14:15; Romans 6:16; D&C 78:7; 132:36; Deuteronomy 4:1–40 (we should obey God)
- 2 Nephi 31:7 (Jesus Christ was obedient)
- Proverbs 3:1–4; 6:20–22; 7:1–3; Ephesians 6:1–3; Colossians 3:20 (children should obey their parents)
- D&C 21:4–6 (obey the prophet)
- John 8:29–32; Mosiah 2:22, 41; D&C 82:10; 1 Nephi 2:20 (blessings for obedience)
- D&C 58:21–22; 98:4–6; 134:5–7 (obey the laws of the land)
- Isaiah 60:12; D&C 1:14; 93:39; 132:6, 39 (consequences of disobedience)
- 2 Nephi 31:16; D&C 53:7; Matthew 24:13; Luke 9:62 (endure to the end)

The Family Can Be Eternal

Chapter 36

The Importance of Families

- Why did our Heavenly Father send us to earth as members of families?

"Marriage between a man and a woman is ordained of God. . . . The family is central to the Creator's plan for the eternal destiny of His children" ("The Family: A Proclamation to the World," *Ensign,* Nov. 1995, 102).

After Heavenly Father brought Adam and Eve together in marriage, He commanded them to have children (see Genesis 1:28). He has revealed that one of the purposes of marriage is to provide mortal bodies for His spirit children. Parents are partners with our Heavenly Father. He wants each of His spirit children to receive a physical body and to experience earth life. When a man and a woman bring children into this world, they help our Heavenly Father carry out His plan.

Every new child should be welcomed into the family with gladness. Each is a child of God. We should take time to enjoy our children, to play with them, and to teach them.

President David O. McKay said, "With all my heart I believe that the best place to prepare for . . . eternal life is in the home" ("Blueprint for Family Living," *Improvement Era,* Apr. 1963, 252). At home, with our families, we can learn self-control, sacrifice, loyalty, and the value of work. We can learn to love, to share, and to serve one another.

For teachers: As you teach this chapter and the next two chapters about families, be sensitive to the feelings of those who do not have ideal situations at home.

Fathers and mothers are responsible to teach their children about Heavenly Father. They should show by example that they love Him because they keep His commandments. Parents should also teach their children to pray and to obey the commandments (see Proverbs 22:6).

- Why is the home the best place to prepare for eternal life?
- How can we help the youth of the Church understand the sacredness of the family and the marriage covenant?

The Eternal Family

Families can be together forever. To enjoy this blessing we must be married in the temple. When people are married outside the temple, the marriage ends when one of the partners dies. When we are married in the temple by the authority of the Melchizedek Priesthood, we are married for time and eternity. If we keep our covenants with the Lord, our families will be united eternally as husband, wife, and children. Death cannot separate us.

Loving Family Relationships

- How can we develop greater harmony in our homes?

Husbands and wives should be thoughtful and kind to each other. They should never do or say anything to hurt each other's feelings. They should also try to do everything possible to make each other happy.

As parents come to know God and strive to be like Him, they will teach children to love one another. In the Book of Mormon, King Benjamin explained:

"Ye will not suffer your children . . . [to] fight and quarrel one with another. . . .

"But ye will teach them to walk in the ways of truth and soberness; ye will teach them to love one another, and to serve one another" (Mosiah 4:14–15).

As family members we can help each other feel confident by giving encouragement and sincere praise. Each child should feel important.

Parents need to show they are interested in what their children do and express love and concern for their children. Children should likewise show their love for their parents. They should be obedient and try to live the kind of life that will bring honor to their parents and to their family name.

- What can parents do to encourage their sons and daughters to be good friends with one another? What can brothers and sisters do to nurture their friendship with one another?
- What can husbands and wives do to help each other be happy?

How to Have a Successful Family

- What are you doing to help strengthen your family and make it successful?

President Harold B. Lee taught, "The most important of the Lord's work you will ever do will be within the walls of your own homes" (*Teachings of Presidents of the Church: Harold B. Lee* [2000], 134).

Satan knows how important families are to our Heavenly Father's plan. He seeks to destroy them by keeping us from drawing near to the Lord. He will tempt us to do things that will draw our families apart.

The First Presidency and Quorum of the Twelve Apostles declared, "Successful marriages and families are established and maintained on principles of faith, prayer, repentance, forgiveness, respect, love, compassion, work, and wholesome recreational activities" (*Ensign,* Nov. 1995, 102).

All of us want to have happy, successful families. The following things will help us achieve this:

1. Have family prayer every night and morning (see 3 Nephi 18:21). Pray together as husband and wife.
2. Teach children the gospel every week in family home evening.
3. Study the scriptures regularly as a family.
4. Do things together as a family, such as work projects, outings, and decision making.

5. Learn to be kind, patient, long-suffering, and charitable (see Moroni 7:45–48).
6. Attend Church meetings regularly (see D&C 59:9–10).
7. Follow the counsel of the Lord in D&C 88:119: "Organize yourselves; prepare every needful thing; and establish a house, even a house of prayer, a house of fasting, a house of faith, a house of learning, a house of glory, a house of order, a house of God."
8. Keep a family history, perform temple work together, and receive the sealing ordinances of the temple.

The family is the most important unit in The Church of Jesus Christ of Latter-day Saints. The Church exists to help families gain eternal blessings and exaltation. The organizations and programs within the Church are designed to strengthen us individually and help us live as families forever.

- What can families do to work through difficult times?
- What evidence have you seen that efforts such as family prayer, family scripture study, family councils, family meal times, and family home evening make a difference?

Additional Scriptures and Other Sources

- Moses 2:27–28 (man and woman created and blessed)
- Genesis 2:24 (man to cleave unto his wife)
- D&C 49:15–16 (God ordained marriage)
- Ephesians 6:4 (train children in righteousness)
- D&C 132:15–21 (eternal marriage)
- D&C 88:119–26 (instructions for a successful family)
- D&C 93:40–50 (the Lord commands parents to bring up their children in light and truth)
- "The Family: A Proclamation to the World" (available on LDS.org and in many Church publications, including *Ensign,* Nov. 1995, page 102; *For the Strength of Youth: Fulfilling Our Duty to God* [item number 36550], page 44; and *True to the Faith: A Gospel Reference* [item number 36863], pages 59–61)

Family Responsibilities

Chapter 37

Responsibilities of the Parents

- What responsibilities do husbands and wives share in raising their children?

Each person has an important place in his or her family. Through prophets the Lord has explained how fathers, mothers, and children should behave and feel toward one another. As husbands, wives, and children, we need to learn what the Lord expects us to do to fulfill our purpose as a family. If we all do our part, we will be united eternally.

In the sacred responsibilities of parenthood, "fathers and mothers are obligated to help one another as equal partners" ("The Family: A Proclamation to the World," *Ensign,* Nov. 1995, 102). They should work together to provide for the spiritual, emotional, intellectual, and physical needs of the family.

Some responsibilities must be shared by the husband and the wife. Parents should teach their children the gospel. The Lord warned that if parents do not teach their children about faith, repentance, baptism, and the gift of the Holy Ghost, the sin will be upon the heads of the parents. Parents should also teach their children to pray and to obey the Lord's commandments. (See D&C 68:25, 28.)

One of the best ways parents can teach their children is by example. Husbands and wives should show love and respect for each other and for their children by both actions and words. It is important to remember that each member of the family is a child of God. Parents should treat their children with love and respect, being firm but kind to them.

For teachers: As with chapter 36, be sensitive to the feelings of those who do not have ideal situations at home. Emphasize that with guidance from the Lord and help from family members and the Church, single parents can successfully raise their children.

Parents should understand that sometimes children will make wrong choices even after they have been taught the truth. When this happens, parents should not give up. They should continue to teach their children, to express love for them, to be good examples to them, and to fast and pray for them.

The Book of Mormon tells us how the prayers of a father helped a rebellious son return to the ways of the Lord. Alma the Younger had fallen away from the teachings of his righteous father, Alma, and had gone about seeking to destroy the Church. The father prayed with faith for his son. Alma the Younger was visited by an angel and repented of his evil way of living. He became a great leader of the Church. (See Mosiah 27:8–32.)

Parents can provide an atmosphere of reverence and respect in the home if they teach and guide their children with love. Parents should also provide happy experiences for their children.

- How can husbands and wives support each other in their roles? Where can single parents turn for support?

Responsibilities of the Father

- What positive examples have you seen of fathers raising their children?

"By divine design, fathers are to preside over their families in love and righteousness and are responsible to provide the necessities of life and protection for their families" (*Ensign,* Nov. 1995, 102). A worthy father who is a member of the Church has the opportunity to hold the priesthood, making him the priesthood leader of his family. He should guide his family with humility and kindness rather than with force or cruelty. The scriptures teach that those who hold the priesthood should lead others by persuasion, gentleness, love, and kindness (see D&C 121:41–44; Ephesians 6:4).

The father shares the blessings of the priesthood with the members of his family. When a man holds the Melchizedek Priesthood, he can share these blessings by administering to the sick and giving special priesthood blessings. Under the direction of a presiding priesthood leader, he can bless babies, baptize, confirm, and perform priesthood ordinations. He should set a good example for his family by keeping the commandments. He should also make sure the family prays together twice daily and holds family home evening.

The father should spend time with each child individually. He should teach his children correct principles, talk with them about their problems and concerns, and counsel them lovingly. Some good examples are found in the Book of Mormon (see 2 Nephi 1:14–3:25; Alma 36–42).

It is also the father's duty to provide for the physical needs of his family, making sure they have the necessary food, housing, clothing, and education. Even if he is unable to provide all the support himself, he does not give up the responsibility of the care of his family.

Responsibilities of the Mother

- What positive examples have you seen of mothers raising their children?

President David O. McKay said that motherhood is the noblest calling (see *Teachings of Presidents of the Church: David O. McKay* [2003], 156). It is a sacred calling, a partnership with God in bringing His spirit children into the world. Bearing children is one of the greatest of all blessings. If there is no father in the home, the mother presides over the family.

President Boyd K. Packer praised women who were unable to have children of their own yet sought to care for others. He said: "When I speak of mothers, I speak not only of those women who have borne children, but also of those who have fostered children born to others, and of the many women who, without children of their own, have mothered the children of others" (*Mothers* [1977], 8).

Latter-day prophets have taught, "Mothers are primarily responsible for the nurture of their children" (*Ensign,* Nov. 1995, 102). A mother needs to spend time with her children and teach them the gospel. She should play and work with them so they can discover the world around them. She also needs to help her family know how to make the home a pleasant place to be. If she is warm and loving, she helps her children feel good about themselves.

The Book of Mormon describes a group of 2,000 young men who rose to greatness because of the teachings of their mothers (see Alma 53:16–23). Led by the prophet Helaman, they went into battle against their enemies. They had learned to be honest, brave, and trustworthy from their mothers. Their mothers also taught them that if they did not doubt, God would deliver them (see Alma 56:47). They all survived the battle. They expressed faith in the teachings of their mothers, saying, "We do not doubt our mothers knew it" (Alma 56:48). Every mother who has a testimony can have a profound effect on her children.

Responsibilities of the Children

- How do children help their parents build a happy home?

Children share with their parents the responsibilities of building a happy home. They should obey the commandments and cooperate with other family members. The Lord is not pleased when children quarrel (see Mosiah 4:14).

The Lord has commanded children to honor their parents. He said, "Honour thy father and thy mother: that thy days may be long upon the land" (Exodus 20:12). To honor parents means to love and respect them. It also means to obey them. The scriptures tell children to "obey your parents in the Lord: for this is right" (Ephesians 6:1).

President Spencer W. Kimball said that children should learn to work and to share responsibilities in the home and yard. They should be given assignments to keep the house neat and clean. (See *Teachings of Presidents of the Church: Spencer W. Kimball* [2006], 120.)

- What should children do to honor and respect their parents?
- What did your parents do that led you to honor and respect them?

Accepting Responsibilities Brings Blessings

- What can each member of the family do to make home a happy place?

A loving and happy family does not happen by accident. Each person in the family must do his or her part. The Lord has given responsibilities to both parents and children. The scriptures teach that we must be thoughtful, cheerful, and considerate of others. When we speak, pray, sing, or work together, we can enjoy the blessings of harmony in our families. (See Colossians 3.)

- What are some traditions and practices that can make home a happy place?

Additional Scriptures and Other Sources

- Proverbs 22:6 (train up a child)
- Ephesians 6:1–3 (children are to obey parents)
- D&C 68:25–28; Ephesians 6:4 (responsibilities of parents)
- "The Family: A Proclamation to the World," (available on LDS.org and in many Church publications, including *Ensign,* Nov. 1995, page 102; *For the Strength of Youth* [item number 36550], page 44; and *True to the Faith* [item number 36863], pages 59–61)
- *Family Guidebook* (item number 31180)

Eternal Marriage

Chapter 38

Marriage Is Ordained of God

Marriage between a man and a woman is a vital part of God's plan. The Lord has said, "Whoso forbiddeth to marry is not ordained of God, for marriage is ordained of God unto man" (D&C 49:15). Since the beginning, marriage has been a law of the gospel. Marriages are intended to last forever, not just for our mortal lives.

Adam and Eve were married by God before there was any death in the world. They had an eternal marriage. They taught the law of eternal marriage to their children and their children's children. As the years passed, wickedness entered the hearts of the people and the authority to perform this sacred ordinance was taken from the earth. Through the Restoration of the gospel, eternal marriage has been restored to earth.

- Why is it important to know that marriage between a man and a woman is ordained of God?

Eternal Marriage Is Essential for Exaltation

- What is the Lord's doctrine of marriage, and how does it differ from the views of the world?

Many people in the world consider marriage to be only a social custom, a legal agreement between a man and a woman to live together. But to Latter-day Saints, marriage is much more. Our exaltation depends on marriage, along with other principles and ordinances, such as faith, repentance, baptism, and receiving the gift of the Holy Ghost. We believe that marriage is the most sacred relationship that can exist between a man and a woman. This sacred relationship affects our happiness now and in the eternities.

Heavenly Father has given us the law of eternal marriage so we can become like Him. The Lord has said:

"In the celestial glory there are three heavens or degrees;

"And in order to obtain the highest, a man must enter into this order of the priesthood [meaning the new and everlasting covenant of marriage];

"And if he does not, he cannot obtain it" (D&C 131:1–3).

Eternal Marriage Must Be Performed by Proper Authority in the Temple

- Why must a marriage be performed by proper authority in the temple to be eternal?

An eternal marriage must be performed by one who holds the sealing power. The Lord promised, "If a man marry a wife by . . . the new and everlasting covenant . . . by him who is anointed, . . . and if [they] abide in [the Lord's] covenant, . . . it . . . shall be of full force when they are out of the world" (D&C 132:19).

Not only must an eternal marriage be performed by the proper priesthood authority, but it must also be done in one of the holy temples of our Lord. The temple is the only place this holy ordinance can be performed.

In the temple, Latter-day Saint couples kneel at one of the sacred altars in the presence of their family and friends who have received the temple endowment. They make their marriage covenants before God. They are pronounced husband and wife for time and all eternity. This is done by one who holds the holy priesthood of God and has been given the authority to perform this sacred ordinance. He acts under the direction of the Lord and promises the couple the blessings of exaltation. He instructs them in the things they must do to receive these blessings. He reminds them that all blessings depend on obedience to the laws of God.

For teachers: All members, whether married or single, need to understand the doctrine of eternal marriage. However, you should be sensitive to the feelings of adults who are not married. As needed, help class members or family members know that all Heavenly Father's children who are faithful to their covenants in this life will have the opportunity to receive all the blessings of the gospel in the eternities, including the opportunity to have an eternal family.

If we are married by any authority other than by the priesthood in a temple, the marriage is for this life only. After death, the marriage partners have no claim on each other or on their children. An eternal marriage gives us the opportunity to continue as families after this life.

Benefits of an Eternal Marriage

- What are the blessings of an eternal marriage in this life and in eternity?

As Latter-day Saints, we are living with an eternal perspective, not just for the moment. However, we can receive blessings in this life as a result of being married for eternity. Some of those blessings are as follows:

1. We know that our marriage can last forever. Death can part us from one another only temporarily. Nothing can part us forever except our own disobedience. This knowledge helps us work harder to have a happy, successful marriage.
2. We know that our family relationships can continue throughout eternity. This knowledge helps us be careful in teaching and training our children. It also helps us show them greater patience and love. As a result, we should have a happier home.
3. Because we have been married in God's ordained way, we are entitled to an outpouring of the Spirit on our marriage as we remain worthy.

Some of the blessings we can enjoy for eternity are as follows:

1. We can live in the highest degree of the celestial kingdom of God.
2. We can be exalted as God is and receive a fulness of joy.

- How can an eternal perspective influence the way we feel about marriage and families?

We Must Prepare for an Eternal Marriage

- What can we do to help youth prepare for eternal marriage?

President Spencer W. Kimball taught: "Marriage is perhaps the most vital of all the decisions and has the most far-reaching effects, for it has to do not only with immediate happiness, but also with eternal joys. It affects not only the two people involved, but also their families and particularly their children and their children's children down through the many generations. In selecting a companion for life and for eternity, certainly the most careful planning and thinking and praying and fasting should be done to be sure that of all the decisions, this one must not be wrong" (*Teachings of Presidents of the Church: Spencer W. Kimball* [2006], 193).

An eternal marriage should be the goal of every Latter-day Saint. This is true even for those already married by civil law. To prepare for an eternal marriage takes much thought and prayer. Only members of the Church who live righteously are permitted to enter the temple (see D&C 97:15–17). We do not suddenly decide one day that we want to be married in the temple, then enter the temple that day and get married. We must first meet certain requirements.

Before we can go to the temple, we must be active, worthy members of the Church for at least one year. Men must hold the Melchizedek Priesthood. We must be interviewed by the branch president or bishop. If he finds us worthy, he will give us a temple recommend. If we are not worthy, he will counsel with us and help us set goals to become worthy to go to the temple.

After we receive a recommend from our bishop or branch president, we must be interviewed by the stake president or the mission president. We are asked questions like the following in interviews for a temple recommend:

1. Do you have faith in and a testimony of God, the Eternal Father; His Son, Jesus Christ; and the Holy Ghost? Do you have a firm testimony of the restored gospel?
2. Do you sustain the President of The Church of Jesus Christ of Latter-day Saints as the prophet, seer, and revelator? Do you recognize him as the only person on earth authorized to exercise all priesthood keys?
3. Do you live the law of chastity?

4. Are you a full-tithe payer?
5. Do you keep the Word of Wisdom?
6. Are you honest in your dealings with others?
7. Do you strive to keep the covenants you have made, to attend your sacrament and priesthood meetings, and to keep your life in harmony with the laws and commandments of the gospel?

When you ask for a temple recommend, you should remember that entering the temple is a sacred privilege. It is a serious act, not something to be taken lightly.

We must seek earnestly to obey every covenant that we make in the temple. The Lord has said that if we are true and faithful, we will enter into our exaltation. We will become like our Heavenly Father. (See D&C 132:19–20.) Temple marriage is worth any sacrifice. It is a way of obtaining eternal blessings beyond measure.

- What can we do to encourage young people to set a goal to be married in the temple? How can we help them prepare for this?

Additional Scriptures

- Genesis 1:26–28 (we should multiply and replenish the earth)
- Genesis 2:21–24 (the first marriage was performed by God)
- Matthew 19:3–8 (what God has joined)
- D&C 132 (the eternal nature of the marriage law)
- D&C 42:22–26 (marriage vows should be kept)
- Jacob 3:5–7 (husbands and wives should be true to each other)

The Law of Chastity

Chapter 39

A Note to Parents

This chapter includes some parts that are beyond the maturity of young children. It is best to wait until children are old enough to understand sexual relations and procreation before teaching them these parts of the chapter. Our Church leaders have told us that parents are responsible to teach their children about procreation (the process of conceiving and bearing children). Parents must also teach them the law of chastity, which is explained in this chapter.

Parents can begin teaching children to have proper attitudes toward their bodies when children are very young. Talking to children frankly but reverently and using the correct names for the parts and functions of their bodies will help them grow up without unnecessary embarrassment about their bodies.

Children are naturally curious. They want to know how their bodies work. They want to know where babies come from. If parents answer all such questions immediately and clearly so children can understand, children will continue to take their questions to their parents. However, if parents answer questions so that children feel embarrassed, rejected, or dissatisfied, they will probably go to someone else with their questions and perhaps get incorrect ideas and improper attitudes.

It is not wise or necessary, however, to tell children everything at once. Parents need only give them the information they have asked for and can understand. While answering these questions, parents can teach children the importance of respecting their bodies and the bodies of others. Parents should teach children to dress modestly. They should correct the false ideas and vulgar language that children learn from others.

By the time children reach maturity, parents should have frankly discussed procreation with them. Children should understand that these powers are good and were given to us by the Lord. He expects us to use them within the bounds He has given us.

Little children come to earth pure and innocent from Heavenly Father. As parents pray for guidance, the Lord will inspire them to teach children at the right time and in the right way.

The Power of Procreation

- Why should parents teach their children about procreation and chastity? How can they appropriately do this?

God commanded each living thing to reproduce after its own kind (see Genesis 1:22). Reproduction was part of His plan so that all forms of life could continue to exist upon the earth.

Then He placed Adam and Eve on the earth. They were different from His other creations because they were His spirit children. In the Garden of Eden, He brought Adam and Eve together in marriage and commanded them to multiply and replenish the earth (see Genesis 1:28). However, their lives were to be governed by moral laws rather than by instinct.

God wanted His spirit children to be born into families so they could be properly cared for and taught. We, like Adam and Eve, are to provide physical bodies for these spirit children. The First Presidency and Quorum of the Twelve Apostles have stated, "We declare the means by which mortal life is created to be divinely appointed" ("The Family: A Proclamation to the World," *Ensign,* Nov. 1995, 102). God has commanded us that only in marriage between a man and a woman are we to have sexual relations. This commandment is called the law of chastity.

The Law of Chastity

- What is the law of chastity?

We are to have sexual relations only with our spouse to whom we are legally married. No one, male or female, is to have sexual relations before marriage. After marriage, sexual relations are permitted only with our spouse.

To the Israelites the Lord said, "Thou shalt not commit adultery" (Exodus 20:14). Those Israelites who broke this commandment were subject to severe penalties. The Lord has repeated this commandment in the latter days (see D&C 42:24).

We have been taught that the law of chastity encompasses more than sexual intercourse. The First Presidency warned young people of other sexual sins:

"Before marriage, do not do anything to arouse the powerful emotions that must be expressed only in marriage. Do not participate in passionate kissing, lie on top of another person, or touch the private, sacred parts of another person's body, with or without clothing. Do not allow anyone to do that with you. Do not arouse those emotions in your own body" (*For the Strength of Youth* [pamphlet, 2001], 27).

Like other violations of the law of chastity, homosexual behavior is a serious sin. Latter-day prophets have spoken about the dangers of homosexual behavior and about the Church's concern for people who may have such inclinations. President Gordon B. Hinckley said:

"In the first place, we believe that marriage between a man and a woman is ordained of God. We believe that marriage may be eternal through exercise of the power of the everlasting priesthood in the house of the Lord.

"People inquire about our position on those who consider themselves so-called gays and lesbians. My response is that we love them as sons and daughters of God. They may have certain inclinations which are powerful and which may be difficult to control. Most people have inclinations of one kind or another at various times. If they do not act upon these inclinations, then they can go forward as do all other members of the Church. If they violate the law of chastity and the moral standards of the Church, then they are subject to the discipline of the Church, just as others are.

"We want to help these people, to strengthen them, to assist them with their problems and to help them with their difficulties. But we cannot stand idle if they indulge in immoral activity, if they try to uphold and defend and live in a so-called same-sex marriage situation. To permit such would be to make light of the very serious and sacred foundation of God-sanctioned marriage and its very purpose, the rearing of families" (in Conference Report, Oct. 1998, 91; or *Ensign,* Nov. 1998, 71).

Satan Wants Us to Break the Law of Chastity

- What are some ways Satan tempts people to break the law of chastity?

Satan's plan is to deceive as many of us as he can to prevent us from returning to live with our Heavenly Father. One of the most damaging things he can do is entice us to break the law of chastity. He is cunning and powerful. He would like us to believe it is no sin to break this law. Many people have been deceived. We must guard ourselves against evil influences.

Satan attacks the standards of modesty. He wants us to believe that because the human body is beautiful, it is something to flaunt and expose. Our Heavenly Father wants us to keep our bodies covered so that we do not encourage improper thoughts in the minds of others.

Satan not only encourages us to dress immodestly, but he also encourages us to think immoral or improper thoughts. He does this with pictures, movies, stories, jokes, music, and dances that suggest immoral acts. The law of chastity requires that our thoughts as well as our actions be pure. The prophet Alma taught that when we are judged by God, "our thoughts will also condemn us; and in this awful state we shall not dare to look up to our God" (Alma 12:14).

Jesus taught, "Ye have heard that it was said by them of old time, Thou shalt not commit adultery:

"But I say unto you, That whosoever looketh on a woman to lust after her hath committed adultery with her already in his heart" (Matthew 5:27–28).

President Gordon B. Hinckley warned: "You live in a world of terrible temptations. Pornography, with its sleazy filth, sweeps over the earth like a horrible, engulfing tide. It is poison. Do not watch it or read it. It will destroy you if you do. It will take from you your self-respect. It will rob you of a sense of the beauties of life. It will tear you down and pull you into a slough of evil thoughts and possibly of evil actions. Stay away from it. Shun it as you would a foul disease, for it is just as deadly. Be virtuous in thought and in deed. God has planted in you, for a purpose, a divine urge which may be easily subverted to evil and destructive ends. When you are young, do not get involved in steady dating. When you reach an age where you think of marriage, then is the time to become so involved. But you boys who are in high school don't need this, and neither do the girls" (in Conference Report, Oct. 1997, 71–72; or *Ensign,* Nov. 1997, 51).

Satan sometimes tempts us through our emotions. He knows when we are lonely, confused, or depressed. He chooses this time of weakness to tempt us to break the law of chastity. Our Heavenly Father can give us the strength to pass through these trials unharmed.

The scriptures tell about a righteous young man named Joseph who was greatly trusted by his master, Potiphar. Potiphar had given Joseph command over everything he had. Potiphar's wife lusted after Joseph and tempted him to commit adultery with her. But Joseph resisted her and fled from her. (See Genesis 39:1–18.)

Paul taught, "There hath no temptation taken you but such as is common to man: but God is faithful, who will not suffer you to be tempted above that ye are able; but will with the temptation also make a way to escape, that ye may be able to bear it" (1 Corinthians 10:13). Alma emphasized that we will "not be tempted above that which [we] can bear" as we "humble [ourselves] before the Lord, and call on his holy name, and watch and pray continually" (Alma 13:28).

- How are modesty and chastity related? How can parents teach their children to be modest in dress, language, and behavior?

For teachers: For help with questions about modesty and chastity, you may want to refer to the pamphlet titled *For the Strength of Youth* (item number 36550), which is available at distribution centers and at LDS.org and which may be available at your meetinghouse library.

- How can we fight the spread and influence of pornography?
- What promises has the Lord given us to help us overcome Satan's temptations?

Breaking the Law of Chastity Is Extremely Serious

The prophet Alma grieved because one of his sons had broken the law of chastity. Alma said to his son Corianton, "Know ye not, my son, that these things are an abomination in the sight of the Lord; yea, most abominable above all sins save it be the shedding of innocent blood or denying the Holy Ghost?" (Alma 39:5). Unchastity is next to murder in seriousness.

If a man and a woman break the law of chastity and conceive a child, they may be tempted to commit another abominable sin: abortion. There is seldom any justifiable reason for abortion. Church leaders have said that some exceptional circumstances may justify an abortion, such as when pregnancy is the result of incest or rape, when the life or health of the mother is judged by competent medical authority to be in serious jeopardy, or when the fetus is known by competent medical authority to have severe defects that will not allow the baby to survive beyond birth. But even these circumstances do not automatically justify an abortion. Those who face such circumstances should consider abortion only after consulting with their local Church leaders and receiving a confirmation through earnest prayer.

"When a man and woman conceive a child out of wedlock, every effort should be made to encourage them to marry. When the probability of a successful marriage is unlikely due to age or other circumstances, unwed parents should be counseled to place the child for adoption through LDS Family Services to ensure that the baby will be sealed to temple-worthy parents" (First Presidency letter, June 26, 2002, and July 19, 2002).

It is extremely important to our Heavenly Father that His children obey the law of chastity. Members of the Church who break this law or influence others to do so are subject to Church discipline.

Those Who Break the Law of Chastity Can Be Forgiven

Peace can come to those who have broken the law of chastity. The Lord tells us, "If the wicked will turn from all his sins that he hath committed, and keep all my statutes, . . . all his transgressions that he hath committed, they shall not be mentioned unto him" (Ezekiel 18:21–22). Peace comes only through forgiveness.

President Kimball said: "To every forgiveness there is a condition. . . . The fasting, the prayers, the humility must be equal to or greater than the sin. There must be a broken heart and a contrite spirit. . . . There must be tears and genuine change of heart. There must be conviction of the sin, abandonment of the evil, confession of the error to properly constituted authorities of the Lord" (*The Miracle of Forgiveness* [1969], 353).

For many people, confession is the most difficult part of repentance. We must confess not only to the Lord but also to the person we have offended, such as a husband or wife, and to the proper priesthood authority. The priesthood leader (bishop or stake president) will judge our standing in the Church. The Lord told Alma, "Whosoever transgresseth against me . . . if he confess his sins before thee and me, and repenteth in the sincerity of his heart, him shall ye forgive, and I will forgive him also" (Mosiah 26:29).

But President Kimball warned: "Even though forgiveness is so abundantly promised there is no promise nor indication of forgiveness to any soul who does not totally repent. . . . We can hardly be too forceful in reminding people that they cannot sin and be forgiven and then sin again and again and expect repeated forgiveness" (*The Miracle of Forgiveness,* 353, 360). Those who receive forgiveness and then repeat the sin are held accountable for their former sins (see D&C 82:7; Ether 2:15).

Those Who Keep the Law of Chastity Are Greatly Blessed

- What blessings do we receive as we keep the law of chastity?

When we obey the law of chastity, we can live without guilt or shame. Our lives and our children's lives are blessed when we keep ourselves pure and spotless before the Lord. Children can look to our example and follow in our footsteps.

Additional Scriptures

- Matthew 19:5–9; Genesis 2:24 (marriage relationship is sacred)
- Titus 2:4–12 (instructions for chastity)
- 1 Corinthians 7:2–5; Ephesians 5:28 (loyalty to spouse)
- Revelation 14:4–5 (blessings for obedience to the law of chastity)
- Proverbs 31:10 (virtue praised)
- Alma 39:9 (do not go after the lusts of your eyes)
- D&C 121:45 (let virtue garnish thy thoughts unceasingly)
- Alma 42:16 (repentance does not come without punishment)
- Alma 42:30 (do not excuse yourself for sinning)
- D&C 58:42–43 (the repentant confess and forsake their sins)

Temple Work and Family History

Chapter 40

Heavenly Father Wants His Children to Return to Him

The Atonement of Jesus Christ assures each of us that we will be resurrected and live forever. But if we are to live forever with our families in Heavenly Father's presence, we must do all that the Savior commands us to do. This includes being baptized and confirmed and receiving the ordinances of the temple.

As members of The Church of Jesus Christ of Latter-day Saints, we have each been baptized and confirmed by one having the proper priesthood authority. Each of us may also go to the temple to receive the saving priesthood ordinances performed there. But many of God's children have not had these same opportunities. They lived at a time or place when the gospel was not available to them.

Heavenly Father wants all of His children to return and live with Him. For those who died without baptism or the temple ordinances, He has provided a way for this to happen. He has asked us to perform ordinances for our ancestors in the temples.

Temples of the Lord

- Why are temples important in our lives?

Temples of The Church of Jesus Christ of Latter-day Saints are special buildings dedicated to the Lord. Worthy Church members may go there to receive sacred ordinances and make covenants with God. Like baptism, these ordinances and covenants are necessary for our salvation. They must be performed in the temples of the Lord.

For teachers: Pictures can generate interest and help learners increase their understanding. Consider asking class members or family members to ponder their feelings about temple work as they look at the picture of a temple in this chapter.

We also go to the temple to learn more about Heavenly Father and His Son, Jesus Christ. We gain a better understanding of our purpose in life and our relationship with Heavenly Father and Jesus Christ. We are taught about our premortal existence, the meaning of earth life, and life after death.

Temple Ordinances Seal Families Together Forever

- What does it mean to be sealed?

All temple ordinances are performed by the power of the priesthood. Through this power, ordinances performed on earth are sealed, or bound, in heaven. The Savior taught His Apostles, "Whatsoever thou shalt bind on earth shall be bound in heaven" (Matthew 16:19; see also D&C 132:7).

Only in the temple can we be sealed together forever as families. Marriage in the temple joins a man and woman as husband and wife eternally if they honor their covenants. Baptism and all other ordinances prepare us for this sacred event.

When a man and woman are married in the temple, their children who are born thereafter also become part of their eternal family. Couples who have been married civilly can receive these blessings by preparing themselves and their children to go to the temple and be sealed to each other. Parents who adopt children legally may have those children sealed to them.

- What must a couple do to make the sealing power effective in their marriage?

Our Ancestors Need Our Help

- What responsibilities do we have toward our ancestors who have died without receiving priesthood ordinances?

Mario Cannamela married Maria Vitta in 1882. They lived in Tripani, Italy, where they raised a family and shared many wonderful years together. Mario and Maria did not hear the message of the restored gospel of Jesus Christ during their lifetimes. They were not baptized. They did not have the opportunity to go to the temple and be sealed together as an eternal family. At death, their marriage ended.

If it is not possible for us to go to the temple to participate in the ordinances, the temple will arrange to have the ordinances performed by other Church members.

- How has the Lord helped you or members of your family find information about your ancestors?

Additional Family History Opportunities

- What are some simple ways for someone with many other responsibilities to participate in family history work?

In addition to providing temple ordinances for the ancestors we know about, we can help those in the spirit world in many other ways. We should seek the guidance of the Spirit as we prayerfully consider what we might do. Depending on our circumstances, we can do the following things:

1. Attend the temple as often as possible. After we have gone to the temple for ourselves, we can perform the saving ordinances for others waiting in the spirit world.
2. Do research to identify ancestors who are more difficult to find. Family history consultants can guide us to helpful resources.
3. Help with the Church's indexing program. Through this program, members prepare genealogical information for use in the Church's family history computer programs. These programs make it easier for us to identify our ancestors.
4. Contribute family history information to the Church's current computer programs for family history. These programs contain genealogies contributed by people all over the world. They allow people to share their family information. Family history consultants can provide more information about the Church's computer programs.
5. Participate in family organizations. We can accomplish much more for our ancestors as we work together with other family members.

- Think about what you can do to increase your participation in temple and family history work.

Additional Scriptures

- 1 Peter 4:6 (gospel was preached to the dead)
- Malachi 4:5–6; D&C 2:2; 3 Nephi 25:5–6 (mission of Elijah)
- 1 Corinthians 15:29; D&C 128:15–18 (work for the dead)
- D&C 138 (redemption of the dead)

The Postmortal Spirit World

Chapter 41

Life after Death

- What happens to us after we die?

Heavenly Father prepared a plan for our salvation. As part of this plan, He sent us from His presence to live on earth and receive mortal bodies of flesh and blood. Eventually our mortal bodies will die, and our spirits will go to the spirit world. The spirit world is a place of waiting, working, learning, and, for the righteous, resting from care and sorrow. Our spirits will live there until we are ready for our resurrection. Then our mortal bodies will once more unite with our spirits, and we will receive the degree of glory we have prepared for (see chapter 46 in this book).

Many people have wondered what the spirit world is like. The scriptures and latter-day prophets have given us information about the spirit world.

- What comfort do you receive from your knowledge that there is life after death? How can we use our understanding of the postmortal spirit world to comfort others?

Where Is the Postmortal Spirit World?

Latter-day prophets have said that the spirits of those who have died are not far from us. President Ezra Taft Benson said: "Sometimes the veil between this life and the life beyond becomes very thin. Our loved ones who have passed on are not far from us" (in Conference Report, Apr. 1971, 18; or *Ensign,* June 1971, 33). President Brigham Young taught that the postmortal spirit world is on the earth, around us (see *Teachings of Presidents of the Church: Brigham Young* [1997], 279).

What Is the Nature of Our Spirits?

Spirit beings have the same bodily form as mortals except that the spirit body is in perfect form (see Ether 3:16). Spirits carry with them from earth their attitudes of devotion or antagonism toward things of righteousness (see Alma 34:34). They have the same appetites and desires that they had when they lived on earth. All spirits are in adult form. They were adults before their mortal existence, and they are in adult form after death, even if they die as infants or children (see *Teachings of Presidents of the Church: Joseph F. Smith* [1998], 131–32).

- Why is it important to know that our spirits will have the same attitudes in the spirit world that they have now?

What Are the Conditions in the Postmortal Spirit World?

The prophet Alma in the Book of Mormon taught about two divisions or states in the spirit world:

"The spirits of those who are righteous are received into a state of happiness, which is called paradise, a state of rest, a state of peace, where they shall rest from all their troubles and from all care, and sorrow.

"And then shall it come to pass, that the spirits of the wicked, yea, who are evil—for behold, they have no part nor portion of the Spirit of the Lord; for behold, they chose evil works rather than good; therefore the spirit of the devil did enter into them, and take possession of their house—and these shall be cast out into outer darkness; there shall be weeping, and wailing, and gnashing of teeth, and this because of their own iniquity, being led captive by the will of the devil.

"Now this is the state of the souls of the wicked, yea, in darkness, and a state of awful, fearful looking for the fiery indignation of the wrath of God upon them; thus they remain in this state, as well as the righteous in paradise, until the time of their resurrection" (Alma 40:12–14).

The spirits are classified according to the purity of their lives and their obedience to the will of the Lord while on earth. The righteous and the wicked are separated (see 1 Nephi 15:28–30), but the spirits may progress as they learn gospel principles and live in accordance with them. The spirits in paradise can teach the spirits in prison (see D&C 138).

Paradise

According to the prophet Alma, the righteous spirits rest from earthly care and sorrow. Nevertheless, they are occupied in doing the work of the Lord. President Joseph F. Smith saw in a vision that immediately after Jesus Christ was crucified, He visited the righteous in the spirit world. He appointed messengers, gave them power and authority, and commissioned them to "carry the light of the gospel to them that were in darkness, even to all the spirits of men" (D&C 138:30).

The Church is organized in the spirit world, and priesthood holders continue their responsibilities there (see D&C 138:30). President Wilford Woodruff taught: "The same Priesthood exists on the other side of the veil. . . . Every Apostle, every Seventy, every Elder, etc., who has died in the faith as soon as he passes to the other side of the veil, enters into the work of the ministry" (*Deseret News,* Jan. 25, 1882, 818).

Family relationships are also important. President Jedediah M. Grant, a counselor to Brigham Young, saw the spirit world and described to Heber C. Kimball the organization that exists there: "He said that the people he there saw were organized in family capacities. . . . He said, 'When I looked at families, there was a deficiency in some, . . . for I saw families that would not be permitted to come and dwell together, because they had not honored their calling here' " (*Deseret News,* Dec. 10, 1856, 316–17).

For teachers: To help class members or family members understand the differences between paradise and spirit prison, consider drawing a vertical line in the middle of the board or on a large piece of paper, making two columns. At the top of one column, write *State of the Righteous.* At the top of the other column, write *State of the Wicked.* Ask members to describe each state in the spirit world, based on their reading in this section. Summarize their comments in the appropriate columns.

Spirit Prison

The Apostle Peter referred to the postmortal spirit world as a prison, which it is for some (see 1 Peter 3:18–20). In the spirit prison are the spirits of those who have not yet received the gospel of Jesus Christ. These spirits have agency and may be enticed by both good and evil. If they accept the gospel and the ordinances performed for them in the temples, they may leave the spirit prison and dwell in paradise.

Also in the spirit prison are those who rejected the gospel after it was preached to them either on earth or in the spirit prison. These spirits suffer in a condition known as hell. They have removed themselves from the mercy of Jesus Christ, who said, "Behold, I, God, have suffered these things for all, that they might not suffer if they would repent; but if they would not repent they must suffer even as I; which suffering caused myself, even God, the greatest of all, to tremble because of pain, and to bleed at every pore, and to suffer both body and spirit" (D&C 19:16–18). After suffering for their sins, they will be allowed, through the Atonement of Jesus Christ, to inherit the lowest degree of glory, which is the telestial kingdom.

- How are conditions in the spirit world similar to conditions in this life?

Additional Scriptures

- 1 Peter 4:6 (gospel preached to the dead)
- Moses 7:37–39 (spirit prison prepared for the wicked)
- D&C 76 (revelation about the three kingdoms of glory)
- Luke 16:19–31 (fate of beggar and rich man in the spirit world)

The Gathering of the House of Israel

Chapter 42

The House of Israel Are God's Covenant People

- What responsibilities do God's covenant people have to the nations of the world?

Jacob was a great prophet who lived hundreds of years before the time of Christ. Because Jacob was faithful, the Lord gave him the special name of Israel, which means "one who prevails with God" or "let God prevail" (Bible Dictionary, "Israel," 708). Jacob had twelve sons. These sons and their families became known as the twelve tribes of Israel, or Israelites (see Genesis 49:28).

Jacob was a grandson of Abraham. The Lord made an everlasting covenant with Abraham that was renewed with Isaac and with Jacob and his children (see chapter 15 in this book; see also the visual in this chapter, depicting Jacob blessing his sons). God promised that the Israelites would be His covenant people as long as they would obey His commandments (see Deuteronomy 28:9–10). They would be a blessing to all the nations of the world by taking the gospel and the priesthood to them (see Abraham 2:9–11). Thus, they would keep their covenant with the Lord and He would keep His covenant with them.

The House of Israel Was Scattered

Again and again prophets of the Lord warned the house of Israel what would happen if they were wicked. Moses prophesied, "And the Lord shall scatter thee among all people, from the one end of the earth even unto the other" (Deuteronomy 28:64).

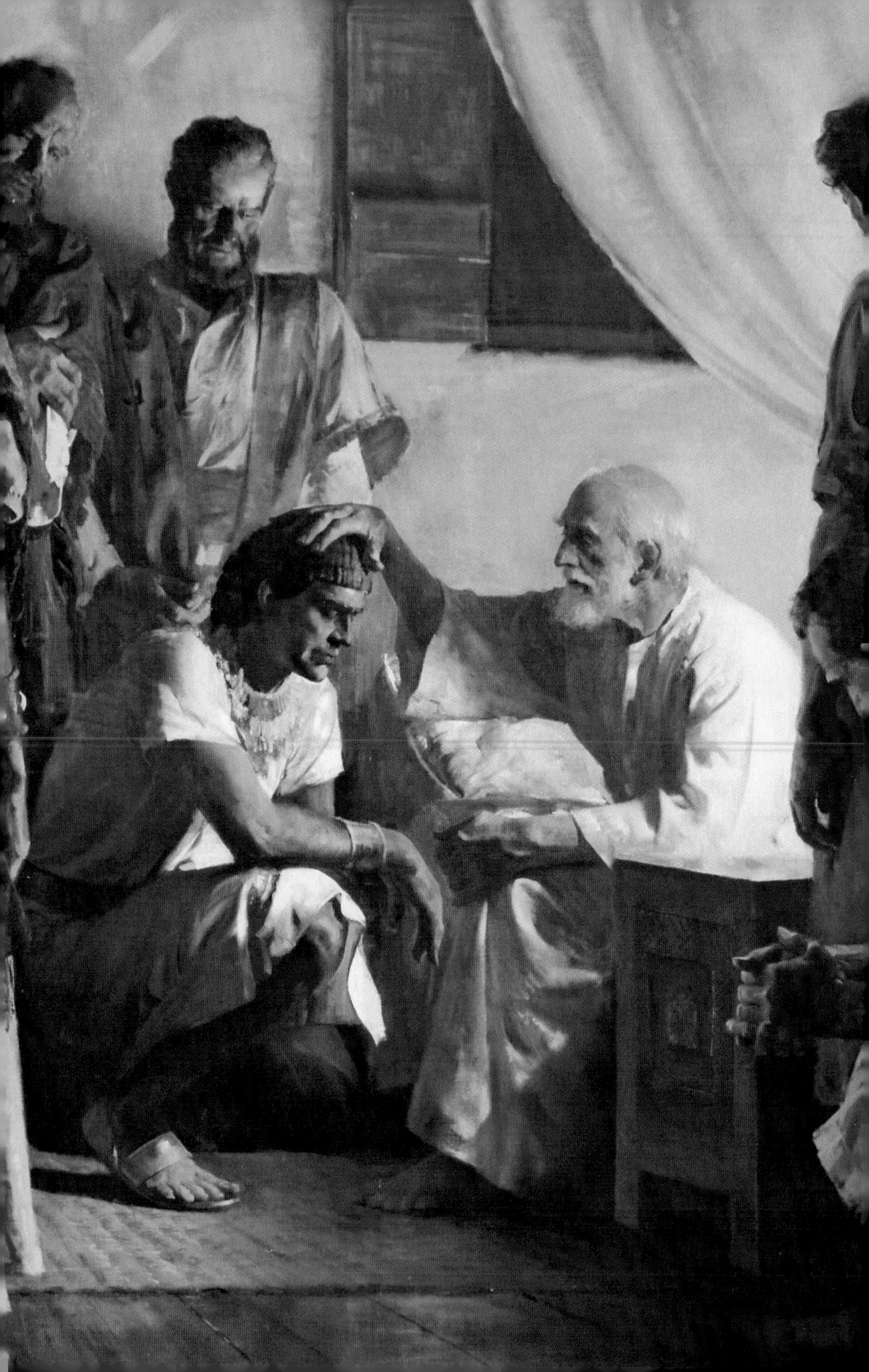

Despite this warning, the Israelites consistently broke the commandments of God. They fought among themselves and split into two kingdoms: the Northern Kingdom, called the kingdom of Israel, and the Southern Kingdom, called the kingdom of Judah. Ten of the twelve tribes of Israel lived in the Northern Kingdom. During a war they were conquered by their enemies and carried away into captivity. Some of them later escaped into the lands of the north and became lost to the rest of the world.

About 100 years after the capture of the Northern Kingdom, the Southern Kingdom was conquered. The capital city of Jerusalem was destroyed in 586 B.C., and many members of the remaining two tribes of Israel were taken captive. Later, some of the members of these tribes returned and rebuilt Jerusalem. Just before Jerusalem was destroyed, Lehi and his family, who were members of the house of Israel, left the city and settled in the Americas.

After the time of Christ, Jerusalem was again destroyed, this time by Roman soldiers. The Jews were scattered over much of the world. Today Israelites are found in all countries of the world. Many of these people do not know that they are descended from the ancient house of Israel.

- What benefits have come to God's children because His covenant people have been scattered throughout the earth?

The House of Israel Must Be Gathered

- Why does the Lord want His people to be gathered?
- How will the house of Israel be gathered?

The Lord promised that His covenant people would someday be gathered: "I will gather the remnant of my flock out of all countries whither I have driven them" (Jeremiah 23:3).

God gathers His children through missionary work. As people come to a knowledge of Jesus Christ, receiving the ordinances of salvation and keeping the associated covenants, they become "the children of the covenant" (3 Nephi 20:26). He has important reasons for gathering His children. He gathers them so they can learn the teachings of the gospel and prepare themselves to meet the Savior when He comes again. He gathers them so they will build temples and perform sacred ordinances for ancestors who have died without having this opportunity. He gathers them so they can strengthen one another and be unified in the gospel, finding protection from unrighteous influences in the world. He also gathers them so they can prepare themselves to share the gospel with others.

The power and authority to direct the work of gathering the house of Israel was given to Joseph Smith by the prophet Moses, who appeared in 1836 in the Kirtland Temple (see D&C 110:11). Since that time, each prophet has held the keys for the gathering of the house of Israel, and this gathering has been an important part of the Church's work. The covenant people are now being gathered as they accept the restored gospel and serve the God of Abraham, Isaac, and Jacob (see Deuteronomy 30:1–5).

The Israelites are to be gathered spiritually first and then physically. They are gathered spiritually as they join The Church of Jesus Christ of Latter-day Saints and make and keep sacred covenants. This spiritual gathering began during the time of the Prophet Joseph Smith and continues today all over the world. Converts to the Church are Israelites either by blood or adoption. They belong to the family of Abraham and Jacob (see Abraham 2:9–11; Galatians 3:26–29).

President Joseph Fielding Smith said: "There are many nations represented in the . . . Church. . . . They have come because the Spirit of the Lord rested upon them; . . . receiving the *spirit of gathering,* they left everything for the sake of the gospel" (*Doctrines of Salvation,* comp. Bruce R. McConkie, 3 vols. [1954–56], 3:256; italics in original).

The physical gathering of Israel means that the covenant people will be "gathered home to the lands of their inheritance, and shall be established in all their lands of promise" (2 Nephi 9:2). The tribes of Ephraim and Manasseh will be gathered in the Americas. The tribe of Judah will return to the city of Jerusalem and the area surrounding it. The ten lost tribes will receive from the tribe of Ephraim their promised blessings (see D&C 133:26–34).

When the Church was first established, the Saints were instructed to gather in Ohio, then Missouri, and then the Salt Lake Valley. Today, however, modern prophets have taught that Church members are to build up the kingdom of God in their own lands. Elder Russell M. Nelson said: "The choice to come unto Christ is not a matter of physical location; it is a matter of individual commitment. People can be 'brought to the knowledge of the Lord' [3 Nephi 20:13] without leaving their homelands. True, in the early days of the Church, conversion often meant emigration as well. But now the gathering takes place in each nation. . . . The place of gathering for Brazilian Saints is in Brazil; the place of gathering for Nigerian Saints is in Nigeria; the place of gathering for Korean Saints is in Korea; and so forth. Zion is 'the pure in heart.' [D&C 97:21.] Zion is wherever righteous Saints are" (in Conference Report, Oct. 2006, 85; or *Ensign,* Nov. 2006, 81).

The physical gathering of Israel will not be complete until the Second Coming of the Savior and on into the Millennium (see Joseph Smith—Matthew 1:37). Then the Lord's promise will be fulfilled:

"Behold, the days come, saith the Lord, that it shall no more be said, The Lord liveth, that brought up the children of Israel out of the land of Egypt;

"But, The Lord liveth, that brought up the children of Israel from the land of the north, and from all the lands whither he had driven them: and I will bring them again into their land that I gave unto their fathers" (Jeremiah 16:14–15).

- In what ways have you been gathered spiritually as one of the Lord's covenant people?
- In what ways have you participated in the gathering of others?

Additional Scriptures

- Genesis 17:1–8 (God's covenant with Abraham)
- Romans 9:4–8; Galatians 3:29 (those who follow Jesus Christ and His word are the children of the covenant)

For teachers: When people share their stories of being converted to the restored gospel of Jesus Christ, they are sharing stories about being gathered spiritually. Consider asking a few people in advance to tell about how they were converted to the gospel.

- 2 Nephi 30:2; Mosiah 5:10–11 (those who repent, follow the prophets, and have faith in Jesus Christ become the Lord's covenant people)
- 2 Kings 17 (Northern Kingdom taken captive)
- 2 Chronicles 36:11–20 (Southern Kingdom taken captive)
- James 1:1 (twelve tribes scattered abroad)
- 1 Nephi 10:12–13 (Nephite migration was part of the scattering)
- Jeremiah 3:14–18 (one from a city, two from a family)
- Ezekiel 20:33–36 (Israel will be gathered from all countries)
- 3 Nephi 20:29–46 (Jews will be gathered to Jerusalem)
- 1 Nephi 15:13–18; 3 Nephi 21:26–29 (gathering starts with Restoration of the gospel)
- D&C 38:31–33 (the Lord's covenant people will be saved)
- Isaiah 11:11–13 (the Lord will recover His people)
- Revelation 18:4–8 (a voice will proclaim the gathering)
- D&C 133:6–15 (Gentiles to Zion, Jews to Jerusalem)

Signs of the Second Coming

Chapter 43

Jesus Christ Will Return to the Earth

• What are some of the signs of the Second Coming?

The Savior told Joseph Smith, "I will reveal myself from heaven with power and great glory . . . and dwell in righteousness with men on earth a thousand years, and the wicked shall not stand" (D&C 29:11; see also chapters 44 and 45 in this book). Jesus has told us that certain signs and events will warn us when the time of His Second Coming is near.

For thousands of years, followers of Jesus Christ have looked forward to the Second Coming as a time of peace and joy. But before the Savior comes, the people of the earth will experience great trials and calamities. Our Heavenly Father wants us to be prepared for these troubles. He also expects us to be spiritually ready when the Savior comes in His glory. Therefore, He has given us signs, which are events that will tell us when the Savior's Second Coming is near. Throughout the ages God has revealed these signs to His prophets. He has said that all faithful followers of Christ will know what the signs are and will be watching for them (see D&C 45:39). If we are obedient and faithful, we will study the scriptures and know of the signs.

Some of the signs foretelling the Second Coming of Jesus Christ have already been or are now being fulfilled. Others will be fulfilled in the future.

For teachers: Consider assigning each class member or family member one or two of the signs described in this chapter (in large classes, some signs may be assigned to more than one person). As part of the lesson, give them time on their own to study the information about those signs and think about evidence they have seen that the signs are being fulfilled today. Then have them share their insights with each other.

Wickedness, War, and Turmoil

Many of the signs are terrifying and dreadful. The prophets have warned that the earth will experience great turmoil, wickedness, war, and suffering. The prophet Daniel said that the time before the Second Coming would be a time of trouble such as the earth has never known (see Daniel 12:1). The Lord said, "The love of men shall wax cold, and iniquity shall abound" (D&C 45:27). "And all things shall be in commotion; and . . . fear shall come upon all people" (D&C 88:91). We can expect earthquakes, disease, famines, great storms, lightnings, and thunder (see Matthew 24:7; D&C 88:90). Hailstorms will destroy the crops of the earth (see D&C 29:16).

Jesus told His disciples that war would fill the earth: "Ye shall hear of wars and rumours of wars. . . . For nation shall rise against nation, and kingdom against kingdom" (Matthew 24:6–7). The Prophet Joseph Smith said: "Be not discouraged when we tell you of perilous times, for they must shortly come, for the sword, famine, and pestilence are approaching. There shall be great destructions upon the face of this land, for ye need not suppose that one jot or tittle of the prophecies of all the holy prophets shall fail, and there are many that remain to be fulfilled yet" (*Teachings of Presidents of the Church: Joseph Smith* [2007], 252).

Many of these signs are being fulfilled. Wickedness is everywhere. Nations are constantly at war. Earthquakes and other calamities are occurring. Many people now suffer from devastating storms, drought, hunger, and diseases. We can be certain that these calamities will become more severe before the Lord comes.

However, not all the events preceding the Second Coming are dreadful. Many of them bring joy to the world.

The Restoration of the Gospel

The Lord said, "Light shall break forth among them that sit in darkness, and it shall be the fulness of my gospel" (D&C 45:28). Prophets of old foretold the Restoration of the gospel. The Apostle John saw that the gospel would be restored by an angel (see Revelation 14:6–7). In fulfillment of this prophecy, the angel

Moroni and other heavenly visitors brought the gospel of Jesus Christ to Joseph Smith.

The Coming Forth of the Book of Mormon

The Lord told the Nephites of another sign: the Book of Mormon would come to their descendants (see 3 Nephi 21). In Old Testament times the prophets Isaiah and Ezekiel foresaw the coming of the Book of Mormon (see Isaiah 29:4–18; Ezekiel 37:16–20). These prophecies are now being fulfilled. The Book of Mormon has been brought forth and is being taken to all the world.

The Gospel Preached to All the World

Another sign of the last days is that the "gospel of the kingdom shall be preached in all the world for a witness unto all nations" (Matthew 24:14; see also Joseph Smith—Matthew 1:31). All people will hear the fulness of the gospel in their own language (see D&C 90:11). Ever since the Restoration of the Church, missionaries have preached the gospel. The missionary effort has increased until now tens of thousands of missionaries preach in many countries of the world in many languages. Before the Second Coming and during the Millennium, the Lord will provide ways to bring the truth to all nations.

The Coming of Elijah

The prophet Malachi prophesied that before the Savior's Second Coming, the prophet Elijah would be sent to the earth. Elijah would restore the sealing powers so families could be sealed together. He would also inspire people to be concerned about their ancestors and descendants. (See Malachi 4:5–6; D&C 2.) The prophet Elijah came to Joseph Smith in April 1836. Since that time, interest in genealogy and family history has grown. We are also able to perform sealing ordinances in the temples for the living and the dead.

Lehi's Descendants Will Become a Great People

The Lord said that when His coming was near, the Lamanites would become a righteous and respected people. He said, "Before the great day of the Lord shall come, . . . the Lamanites shall blossom as the rose" (D&C 49:24). Great numbers of Lehi's descendants are now receiving the blessings of the gospel.

Building of the New Jerusalem

Near the time of the coming of Jesus Christ, the faithful Saints will build a righteous city, a city of God, called the New Jerusalem. Jesus Christ Himself will rule there. (See 3 Nephi 21:23–25; Moses 7:62–64; Articles of Faith 1:10.) The Lord said the city will be built in the state of Missouri in the United States (see D&C 84:2–3).

These are only a few of the signs that the Lord has given us. The scriptures describe many more.

- What evidence do you see that the signs are being fulfilled?

Knowing the Signs of the Times Can Help Us

- How can we remain calm and at peace even when some of the signs are terrifying and dreadful?

Speaking of His Second Coming, the Lord said, "The hour and the day no man knoweth, neither the angels in heaven" (D&C 49:7). He taught this with the parable of the fig tree. He said that when we see a fig tree putting forth leaves, we can tell that summer will soon come. Likewise, when we see the signs described in the scriptures, we can know that His coming is near. (See Matthew 24:32–33.)

The Lord gives these signs to help us. We can put our lives in order and prepare ourselves and our families for those things yet to come.

We have been warned of calamities and told to prepare for them, but we can also look forward to the coming of the Savior and be glad. The Lord said, "Be not troubled, for, when all these things [the signs] shall come to pass, ye may know that the promises which have been made unto you shall be fulfilled" (D&C 45:35). He said those who are righteous when He comes will not be destroyed "but shall abide the day. And the earth shall be given unto them for an inheritance; . . . and their children shall grow up without sin. . . . For the Lord shall be in their midst, and his glory shall be upon them, and he will be their king and their lawgiver" (D&C 45:57–59).

2. *He will judge His people.* When Jesus comes again, He will judge the nations and will divide the righteous from the wicked (see Matthew 25:31–46; see also chapter 46 in this book). John the Revelator wrote about this judgment: "I saw thrones, and they sat upon them, and judgment was given unto them: and I saw the souls of them that were beheaded for the witness of Jesus, and for the word of God, . . . and they lived and reigned with Christ a thousand years." The wicked he saw "lived not again until the thousand years were finished" (Revelation 20:4–5; see also D&C 88:95–98).

3. *He will usher in the Millennium.* The Millennium is the thousand-year period when Jesus will reign on the earth. The righteous will be caught up to meet Jesus at His coming (see D&C 88:96). His coming will begin the millennial reign. (See chapter 45 in this book.)

   President Brigham Young said:

   "In the Millennium, when the Kingdom of God is established on the earth in power, glory and perfection, and the reign of wickedness that has so long prevailed is subdued, the Saints of God will have the privilege of building their temples, and of entering into them, becoming, as it were, pillars in the temples of God [see Revelation 3:12], and they will officiate for their dead. Then we will see our friends come up, and perhaps some that we have been acquainted with here. . . . And we will have revelations to know our forefathers clear back to Father Adam and Mother Eve, and we will enter into the temples of God and officiate for them. Then [children] will be sealed to [parents] until the chain is made perfect back to Adam, so that there will be a perfect chain of Priesthood from Adam to the winding-up scene" (*Teachings of Presidents of the Church: Brigham Young* [1997], 333–34).

4. *He will complete the First Resurrection.* Those who have obtained the privilege of coming forth in the resurrection of the just will rise from their graves. They will be caught up to meet the Savior as He comes down from heaven. (See D&C 88:97–98.)

After Jesus Christ rose from the dead, other righteous people who had died were also resurrected. They appeared in Jerusalem and also on the American continent. (See Matthew 27:52–53; 3 Nephi 23:9–10.) This was the beginning of the First Resurrection. Some people have been resurrected since then. Those who already have been resurrected and those who will be resurrected at the time of His coming will all inherit the glory of the celestial kingdom (see D&C 76:50–70).

After the resurrection of those who will inherit celestial glory, another group will be resurrected: those who will receive a terrestrial glory. When all these people have been resurrected, the First Resurrection will be completed.

The wicked who are living at the time of the Second Coming of the Lord will be destroyed in the flesh. They, along with the wicked who are already dead, will have to wait until the last resurrection. All of the remaining dead will rise to meet God. They will either inherit the telestial kingdom or be cast into outer darkness with Satan (see D&C 76:32–33, 81–112).

5. *He will take His rightful place as King of heaven and earth.* When Jesus comes, He will establish His government on the earth. The Church will become part of that kingdom. He will rule all the people of the earth in peace for 1,000 years.

   When Jesus Christ first came to the earth, He did not come in glory. He was born in a lowly stable and laid in a manger of hay. He did not come with great armies as the Jews had expected of their Savior. Instead, He came saying, "Love your enemies, . . . do good to them that hate you, and pray for them which despitefully use you" (Matthew 5:44). He was rejected and crucified. But He will not be rejected at His Second Coming, "for every ear shall hear it, and every knee shall bow, and every tongue shall confess" that Jesus is the Christ (D&C 88:104). He will be greeted as "Lord of lords, and King of kings" (Revelation 17:14). He will be called "Wonderful, Counsellor, The mighty God, The everlasting Father, The Prince of Peace" (Isaiah 9:6).

- What are your thoughts and feelings as you contemplate the events of the Second Coming?

How Will We Know When the Savior's Coming Is Near?

When Jesus Christ was born, very few people knew that the Savior of the world had come. When He comes again, there will be no doubt who He is. No one knows the exact time that the Savior will come again. "Of that day and hour knoweth no man, no, not the angels of heaven, but my Father only" (Matthew 24:36; see also D&C 49:7).

The Lord used a parable to give us an idea of the time of His coming:

"Now learn a parable of the fig tree; When her branch is yet tender, and putteth forth leaves, ye know that summer is near:

"So ye in like manner, when ye shall see these things come to pass, know that it is nigh, even at the doors" (Mark 13:28–29).

The Lord has also given us some signs to let us know when His coming is near. After revealing the signs, He cautioned:

"Watch therefore: for ye know not what hour your Lord doth come. . . .

". . . Be ye also ready: for in such an hour as ye think not the Son of man cometh" (Matthew 24:42, 44).

For more information about how we will know when Jesus's Second Coming is near, see chapter 43 in this book.

How Can We Be Ready When the Savior Comes?

The best way we can prepare for the Savior's coming is to accept the teachings of the gospel and make them part of our lives. We should live each day the best we can, just as Jesus taught when He was on the earth. We can look to the prophet for guidance and follow his counsel. We can live worthy to have the Holy Ghost guide us. Then we will look forward to the Savior's coming with happiness and not with fear. The Lord said: "Fear not, little flock, the kingdom is yours until I come. Behold, I come quickly. Even so. Amen" (D&C 35:27).

- Why should we be concerned about our preparedness rather than the exact timing of the Second Coming?

Additional Scriptures

- John 14:2–3; Matthew 26:64 (Jesus to prepare a place and come again)
- Malachi 3:2–3; 4:1; D&C 64:23–24 (earth to be burned)
- D&C 133:41–51 (wicked to be destroyed)
- Matthew 13:40–43 (the Judgment predicted)
- 1 Corinthians 15:40–42; D&C 76; 88:17–35 (kingdoms of glory)
- D&C 43:29–30; 29:11 (the Savior's coming will usher in the Millennium)
- Articles of Faith 1:10 (Jesus to reign)
- Alma 11:43–44; 40:23 (the Resurrection explained)
- D&C 88:96–98 (the dead to rise)
- Zechariah 14:9; Revelation 11:15; 1 Nephi 22:24–26 (Jesus to reign as King)

The Millennium

Chapter 45

People on the Earth during the Millennium

- Who will be on the earth during the Millennium?

A thousand years of peace, love, and joy will begin on the earth at the Second Coming of Jesus Christ. This thousand-year period is called the Millennium. The scriptures and the prophets help us understand what it will be like to live on the earth during the Millennium.

Because of the destruction of the wicked at the Savior's Second Coming, only righteous people will live on the earth at the beginning of the Millennium. They will be those who have lived virtuous and honest lives. These people will inherit either the terrestrial or celestial kingdom.

During the Millennium, mortals will still live on earth, and they will continue to have children as we do now (see D&C 45:58). Joseph Smith said that immortal beings will frequently visit the earth. These resurrected beings will help with the government and other work. (See *Teachings of the Prophet Joseph Smith,* sel. Joseph Fielding Smith [1976], 268.)

People will still have their agency, and for a time many will be free to continue with their religions and ideas. Eventually everyone will confess that Jesus Christ is the Savior.

During the Millennium, Jesus will "reign personally upon the earth" (Articles of Faith 1:10). Joseph Smith explained that Jesus will "reign over the Saints and come down and instruct" (*Teachings of Presidents of the Church: Joseph Smith* [2007], 258).

For teachers: The subject of the Millennium sometimes leads people to speculate about ideas that are not found in the scriptures or the teachings of latter-day prophets. As you guide this lesson, be careful to avoid such speculation.

The Work of the Church during the Millennium

• What are the two great works that will be done during the Millennium?

There will be two great works for members of the Church during the Millennium: temple work and missionary work. Temple work involves the ordinances that are necessary for exaltation. These include baptism, the laying on of hands for the gift of the Holy Ghost, and the temple ordinances—the endowment, temple marriage, and the sealing together of family units.

Many people have died without receiving these ordinances. People on the earth must perform these ordinances for them. This work is now being done in the temples of the Lord. There is too much work to finish before the Millennium begins, so it will be completed during that time. Resurrected beings will help us correct the mistakes we have made in doing research concerning our dead ancestors. They will also help us find the information we need to complete our records. (See Joseph Fielding Smith, *Doctrines of Salvation,* comp. Bruce R. McConkie, 3 vols. [1954–56], 2:167, 251–52.)

The other great work during the Millennium will be missionary work. The gospel will be taught with great power to all people. Eventually there will be no need to teach others the first principles of the gospel because "they shall all know me, from the least of them unto the greatest of them, saith the Lord" (Jeremiah 31:34).

• How can we prepare now for work in the Millennium?

Conditions during the Millennium

• In what ways will life during the Millennium be different from life on the earth now?

The Prophet Joseph Smith taught that during the Millennium, "the earth will be renewed and receive its paradisiacal glory" (Articles of Faith 1:10).

Satan Bound

During the Millennium, Satan will be bound. This means he will not have power to tempt those who are living at that time

The Final Judgment

Chapter 46

Judgments of God

- What are some different judgments that come before the Final Judgment? How do all these judgments relate to one another?

We are often told in the scriptures that the day will come when we will stand before God and be judged. We need to understand how judgment takes place so we can be better prepared for this important event.

The scriptures teach that all of us will be judged according to our works: "And I saw the dead, small and great, stand before God; and the books were opened: and another book was opened, which is the book of life: and the dead were judged out of those things which were written in the books, according to their works" (Revelation 20:12; see also D&C 76:111; 1 Nephi 15:32; Abraham 3:25–28). We will also be judged "according to the desire of [our] hearts" (D&C 137:9; see also Alma 41:3).

Here on earth we are often judged as to our worthiness to receive opportunities within the kingdom of God. When we are baptized we are judged worthy to receive this ordinance. When we are called to serve in the Church or interviewed for a priesthood advancement or a temple recommend, we are judged.

Alma taught that when we die our spirits are assigned to a state of happiness or of misery (see Alma 40:11–15). This is a judgment.

Our Words, Works, and Thoughts Are Used to Judge Us

- Imagine being judged for all your thoughts, words, and actions.

For teachers: You do not need to teach everything in each chapter. As you prayerfully prepare to teach, seek the Spirit's guidance to know which portions of the chapter you should cover.

The prophet Alma testified, "Our words will condemn us, yea, all our works will condemn us; . . . and our thoughts will also condemn us" (Alma 12:14).

The Lord said: "Every idle word that men shall speak, they shall give account thereof in the day of judgment. For by thy words thou shalt be justified, and by thy words thou shalt be condemned" (Matthew 12:36–37).

Faith in Jesus Christ helps us be prepared for the Final Judgment. Through faithful discipleship to Him and repentance of all our sins, we can be forgiven for our sins and become pure and holy so that we can dwell in the presence of God. As we repent of our sins, giving up every impure thought and act, the Holy Ghost will change our hearts so we no longer have even the desire to sin (see Mosiah 5:2). Then when we are judged, we will be found ready to enter into God's presence.

- Think about what you can do to improve your thoughts, words, and actions.

We Will Be Judged by Records

- From what records will we be judged? Who will judge us?

The Prophet Joseph Smith said that the dead will be judged out of records kept on earth. We will also be judged out of the "book of life," which is kept in heaven (see D&C 128:6–8).

"Every one of you . . . must stand before 'the judgment-seat of the Holy One of Israel . . . and then must . . . be judged according to the holy judgment of God.' (II Nephi 9:15.) And according to the vision of John, 'The books were opened: and another book was opened, which is the book of life: and the dead were judged out of those things which were written in the books, according to their works.' (Rev. 20:12.) The 'books' spoken of refer to the 'records [of your works] which are kept on the earth. . . . The book of life is the record which is kept in heaven.' (Doc. and Cov. 128:7.)" (*Teachings of Presidents of the Church: Harold B. Lee* [2000], 226–27).

There is another record that will be used to judge us. The Apostle Paul taught that we ourselves are a record of our life (see Romans 2:15). Stored in our body and mind is a complete history of everything we have done. President John Taylor taught this truth: "[The individual] tells the story himself, and bears witness against himself. . . . That record that is written by the man himself in the tablets of his own mind, that record that cannot lie will in that day be unfolded before God and angels, and those who shall sit as judges" (*Deseret News,* Mar. 8, 1865, 179).

The Apostle John taught that "the Father judgeth no man, but hath committed all judgment unto the Son" (John 5:22). The Son, in turn, will call upon others to assist in the Judgment. The Twelve who were with Him in His ministry will judge the twelve tribes of Israel (see Matthew 19:28; Luke 22:30). The twelve Nephite disciples will judge the Nephite and Lamanite people (see 1 Nephi 12:9–10; Mormon 3:18–19).

Inheriting a Place in a Kingdom of Glory

- How will our faithfulness during our life on earth influence our life in the eternities?

At the Final Judgment we will inherit a place in the kingdom for which we are prepared. The scriptures teach of three kingdoms of glory—the celestial kingdom, the terrestrial kingdom, and the telestial kingdom (see D&C 88:20–32).

In Doctrine and Covenants 76, the Lord described the ways we can choose to live our mortal lives. He explained that our choices will determine which kingdom we are prepared for. We learn from this revelation that even members of the Church will inherit different kingdoms because they will not be equally faithful and valiant in their obedience to Christ.

The following are the kinds of lives we can choose to live and the kingdoms our choices will obtain for us.

- Mormon 3:22 (repent and prepare to stand before the judgment seat)
- Luke 12:47–48; D&C 82:3 (of whom much is given, much is required)
- D&C 88:16–33 (we each receive that for which we are worthy)

Exaltation

Chapter 47

The Plan for Our Progression

When we lived with our Heavenly Father, He explained a plan for our progression. We could become like Him, an exalted being. The plan required that we be separated from Him and come to earth. This separation was necessary to prove whether we would obey our Father's commandments even though we were no longer in His presence. The plan provided that when earth life ended, we would be judged and rewarded according to the degree of our faith and obedience.

From the scriptures we learn that there are three kingdoms of glory in heaven. The Apostle Paul mentioned that he knew a man who was "caught up to the third heaven" (2 Corinthians 12:2). Paul named two of the kingdoms in heaven: the celestial and the terrestrial (see 1 Corinthians 15:40–42). The celestial is the highest, and the terrestrial is second. Through latter-day revelation we learn that the third kingdom is the telestial kingdom (see D&C 76:81). We also learn that there are three heavens or degrees within the celestial kingdom (see D&C 131:1).

Exaltation

- What is exaltation?

Exaltation is eternal life, the kind of life God lives. He lives in great glory. He is perfect. He possesses all knowledge and all wisdom. He is the Father of spirit children. He is a creator. We can become like our Heavenly Father. This is exaltation.

If we prove faithful to the Lord, we will live in the highest degree of the celestial kingdom of heaven. We will become exalted, to live

with our Heavenly Father in eternal families. Exaltation is the greatest gift that Heavenly Father can give His children (see D&C 14:7).

Blessings of Exaltation

- What are some blessings that will be given to those who are exalted?

Our Heavenly Father is perfect, and He glories in the fact that it is possible for His children to become like Him. His work and glory is "to bring to pass the immortality and eternal life of man" (Moses 1:39).

Those who receive exaltation in the celestial kingdom through faith in Jesus Christ will receive special blessings. The Lord has promised, "All things are theirs" (D&C 76:59). These are some of the blessings given to exalted people:

1. They will live eternally in the presence of Heavenly Father and Jesus Christ (see D&C 76:62).
2. They will become gods (see D&C 132:20–23).
3. They will be united eternally with their righteous family members and will be able to have eternal increase.
4. They will receive a fulness of joy.
5. They will have everything that our Heavenly Father and Jesus Christ have—all power, glory, dominion, and knowledge (see D&C 132:19–20). President Joseph Fielding Smith wrote: "The Father has promised through the Son that all that he has shall be given to those who are obedient to His commandments. *They shall increase in knowledge, wisdom, and power, going from grace to grace, until the fulness of the perfect day shall burst upon them*" (*Doctrines of Salvation,* comp. Bruce R. McConkie, 3 vols. [1954–56], 2:36; italics in original).

Requirements for Exaltation

The time to fulfill the requirements for exaltation is now (see Alma 34:32–34). President Joseph Fielding Smith said, "In order to obtain the exaltation we must accept the gospel and all its covenants; and

Page 60: *Not My Will, But Thine, Be Done,* by Harry Anderson. © Seventh-day Adventist Church. Do not copy

Page 82: Detail from *Abraham on the Plains of Mamre,* by Harry Anderson. © IRI

Page 88: Detail from *Christ Ordaining the Twelve Apostles,* by Harry Anderson. © IRI

Page 94: Detail from *The Desires of My Heart,* by Walter Rane. Courtesy Church History Museum

Page 102: Detail from *Jesus Christ,* by Harry Anderson. © IRI

Page 134: *The Last Supper,* by Simon Dewey. © Simon Dewey

Page 150: Detail from *Christ and the Rich Young Ruler,* by Heinrich Hofmann. Courtesy C. Harrison Conroy Co., Inc.

Page 162: Detail from *Jesus Washing the Feet of the Apostles,* by Del Parson. © 1983 IRI

Page 168: Photograph © Getty Images

Page 174: Detail from *The Good Samaritan,* by Joseph Brickey. © 2001 Joseph Brickey

Page 180: Photograph by George Doyle/Stockbyte/Getty Images

Page 190: Detail from *Go Ye Therefore, and Teach All Nations,* by Harry Anderson. © IRI

Page 200: *Adam and Eve Offering Sacrifices,* by Keith Larson. © 1996 Keith Larson

Page 218: Photograph by Robert Casey. © 2004 Robert Casey

Page 224: Photograph by Robert Casey. © 2004 Robert Casey

Page 246: Detail from *Jacob Blessing Joseph,* by Harry Anderson. © IRI

Page 252: *The Second Coming,* by Harry Anderson. © IRI

Page 258: Detail from *The Second Coming,* by Harry Anderson. © IRI

Page 264: Detail from *Without Any Ire,* by Nancy Glazier-Koehler. © 1984 Nancy Glazier-Koehler

Page 268: Detail from *The Last Judgment,* by John Scott. © 1974 IRI

Page 276: Detail from mural by Dan Baxter

Index

A

B

C

D

E

F

G

H

Contents

Introduction

A Study Guide and a Teacher's Manual

Gospel Principles was written both as a personal study guide and as a teacher's manual. As you study it, seeking the Spirit of the Lord, you can grow in your understanding and testimony of God the Father, Jesus Christ and His Atonement, and the Restoration of the gospel. You can find answers to life's questions, gain an assurance of your purpose and self-worth, and face personal and family challenges with faith.

Instructions for Teaching at Church and at Home

Being a teacher is a great responsibility that includes many opportunities to strengthen others and see that they are "nourished by the good word of God" (Moroni 6:4). You will teach effectively as you follow these principles:

- Love those you teach.
- Teach by the Spirit.
- Teach the doctrine.
- Invite diligent learning.

Love Those You Teach

When you show love for those you teach, they become more receptive to the Spirit of the Lord. They become more enthusiastic about learning and more open to you and to others. Strive to become acquainted with those you teach, and let them know that you genuinely care about them. Be sensitive to the challenges of those with special needs. Create a comfortable environment in your class so that participants feel free to call upon you for help with any questions they have about the principles of the gospel and how to apply them.

The Lord's Spirit will be present when love and unity exist. The Lord said, "A new commandment I give unto you, That ye love one another; as I have loved you, that ye also love one another" (John 13:34).

For more on this subject, see *Teaching, No Greater Call,* pages 31–39.

Teach by the Spirit

The most important things you will ever teach are the doctrines of Christ as revealed through the scriptures and modern prophets and as confirmed by the Holy Ghost. To do this effectively, you must obtain the Spirit of the Lord. "The Spirit shall be given unto you by the prayer of faith," said the Lord, "and if ye receive not the Spirit ye shall not teach" (D&C 42:14; see also D&C 50:13–22). The Holy Ghost is the real teacher, so it is important to create an environment in which the Lord's Spirit can be present.

For more on this subject, see *Teaching, No Greater Call,* pages 41–48.

Teach the Doctrine

Before you teach from a chapter, study it thoroughly to be sure you understand the doctrine. Also study the additional scriptures listed at the end of the chapter. You will teach with greater sincerity and power when the teachings in the chapter have influenced you personally. Never speculate about Church doctrine. Teach only what is supported by the scriptures, the words of latter-day prophets and apostles, and the Holy Spirit (see D&C 42:12–14; 52:9).

If you have been called to teach a quorum or class using this book, do not substitute outside materials, however interesting they may be. Stay true to the scriptures and the words in the book. As appropriate, use personal experiences and articles from Church magazines to supplement the lessons.

For more on this subject, see *Teaching, No Greater Call,* pages 50–59.

Invite Diligent Learning

As you teach, help others see how gospel principles apply to daily living. Encourage discussions on how these principles can affect our feelings about God, ourselves, our families, and our neighbors. Encourage participants to live according to the principles.

Try to involve as many people as possible in the lessons. You can do this by inviting them to read aloud, answer questions, or share experiences, but do so only when you are sure it will not embarrass them. You may want to make special assignments to participants while preparing the lessons. Be sensitive to the needs and feelings of others. You may need to talk privately with individuals before a lesson and ask how they feel about participating.

For more on this subject, see *Teaching, No Greater Call,* pages 61–74.

Additional Help for Teachers

Each chapter in this book contains one or two notes for teachers. These notes include ideas that can help you in your efforts to love those you teach, teach by the Spirit, teach the doctrine, and invite diligent learning among those you teach.

Our Heavenly Father

Chapter 1

There Is a God

• What are some things that testify to you that there is a God?

Alma, a Book of Mormon prophet, wrote, "All things denote there is a God; yea, even the earth, and all things that are upon the face of it, yea, and its motion, yea, and also all the planets which move in their regular form do witness that there is a Supreme Creator" (Alma 30:44). We can look up at the sky at night and have an idea of what Alma meant. There are millions of stars and planets, all in perfect order. They did not get there by chance. We can see the work of God in the heavens and on the earth. The many beautiful plants, the many kinds of animals, the mountains, the rivers, the clouds that bring us rain and snow—all these testify to us that there is a God.

The prophets have taught us that God is the Almighty Ruler of the universe. God dwells in heaven (see D&C 20:17). Through His Son, Jesus Christ, He created the heavens and the earth and all things that are in them (see 3 Nephi 9:15; Moses 2:1). He made the moon, the stars, and the sun. He organized this world and gave it form, motion, and life. He filled the air and the water with living things. He covered the hills and plains with all kinds of animal life. He gave us day and night, summer and winter, seedtime and harvest. He made man in His own image to be a ruler over His other creations (see Genesis 1:26–27).

God is the Supreme and Absolute Being in whom we believe and whom we worship. He is "the Great Parent of the universe," and He "looks upon the whole of the human family with a fatherly care

---

For teachers: Use questions at the beginning of a section to start a discussion and send class members or family members to the text to find more information. Use questions at the end of a section to help class members or family members ponder and discuss the meaning of what they have read and apply it in their lives.

and paternal regard" (*Teachings of Presidents of the Church: Joseph Smith* [2007], 39).

The Nature of God

• What are some of God's attributes?

Because we are made in His image (see Moses 2:26; 6:9), we know that our bodies are like His body. His eternal spirit is housed in a tangible body of flesh and bones (see D&C 130:22). God's body, however, is perfected and glorified, with a glory beyond all description.

God is perfect. He is a God of righteousness, with attributes such as love, mercy, charity, truth, power, faith, knowledge, and judgment. He has all power. He knows all things. He is full of goodness.

All good things come from God. Everything that He does is to help His children become like Him. He has said, "Behold, this is my work and my glory—to bring to pass the immortality and eternal life of man" (Moses 1:39).

• Why is it important for us to understand the nature of God?

Coming to Know God

• How can we come to know God?

Knowing God is so important that the Savior said, "This is life eternal, that they might know thee the only true God, and Jesus Christ, whom thou hast sent" (John 17:3).

The first and greatest commandment is "Thou shalt love the Lord thy God with all thy heart" (Matthew 22:37).

The more we know God, the more we love Him and keep His commandments (see 1 John 2:3–5). By keeping His commandments we can become like Him.

We can know God if we will:

1. Believe that He exists and that He loves us (see Mosiah 4:9).
2. Study the scriptures (see 2 Timothy 3:14–17).

3. Pray to Him (see James 1:5).
4. Obey all His commandments as best we can (see John 14:21–23).

As we do these things, we will come to know God and eventually have eternal life.

• Ponder what you can do to draw nearer to God.

Additional Scriptures

- Acts 7:55–56 (Son at the right hand of the Father)
- D&C 88:41–44 (attributes of God)
- Psalm 24:1 (the earth is the Lord's)
- Moses 1:30–39 (Creation)
- Alma 7:20 (God cannot do wrong)
- Joseph Smith—History 1:17 (Father and Son are separate beings)
- Alma 5:40 (good comes from God)
- John 14:6–9 (Son and Father are alike)
- Mormon 9:15–20 (God of miracles)
- Amos 3:7 (God of revelation)
- John 3:16 (God of love)

Our Heavenly Family

Chapter 2

We Are Children of Our Heavenly Father

- What do scriptures and latter-day prophets teach us about our relationship to God?

God is not only our Ruler and Creator; He is also our Heavenly Father. All men and women are literally the sons and daughters of God. "Man, as a spirit, was begotten and born of heavenly parents, and reared to maturity in the eternal mansions of the Father, prior to coming upon the earth in a temporal [physical] body" (*Teachings of Presidents of the Church: Joseph F. Smith* [1998], 335).

Every person who was ever born on earth is our spirit brother or sister. Because we are the spirit children of God, we have inherited the potential to develop His divine qualities. Through the Atonement of Jesus Christ, we can become like our Heavenly Father and receive a fulness of joy.

- How does your knowledge that you are a child of God influence your thoughts, words, and actions?

We Developed Personalities and Talents While We Lived in Heaven

- Think about talents and gifts you have been blessed with.

The scriptures teach us that the prophets prepared themselves to become leaders on earth while they were still spirits in heaven (see Alma 13:1–3). Before they were born into mortal bodies, God foreordained (chose) them to be leaders on earth. Jesus, Adam, and Abraham were some of these leaders. (See Abraham 3:22–23.)

For teachers: You do not need to teach everything in each chapter. As you prayerfully prepare to teach, seek the Spirit's guidance to know which portions of the chapter you should cover and which questions you should ask.

Joseph Smith taught that "every man who has a calling to minister to the inhabitants of the world was [fore]ordained to that very purpose" (*Teachings of Presidents of the Church: Joseph Smith* [2007], 511). However, everyone on earth is free to accept or reject any opportunity to serve.

We were not all alike in heaven. We know, for example, that we were sons and daughters of heavenly parents—males and females (see "The Family: A Proclamation to the World," *Ensign,* Nov. 1995, 102). We possessed different talents and abilities, and we were called to do different things on earth. We can learn more about our "eternal possibilities" when we receive our patriarchal blessings (see Thomas S. Monson, in Conference Report, Oct. 1986, 82; or *Ensign,* Nov. 1986, 66).

A veil covers our memories of our premortal life, but our Father in Heaven knows who we are and what we did before we came here. He has chosen the time and place for each of us to be born so we can learn the lessons we personally need and do the most good with our individual talents and personalities.

- How have other people's talents blessed you? How can your talents and gifts bless others?

Our Heavenly Father Presented a Plan for Us to Become Like Him

- How does earth life help prepare us to become like our Heavenly Father?

Our Heavenly Father knew we could not progress beyond a certain point unless we left Him for a time. He wanted us to develop the godlike qualities that He has. To do this, we needed to leave our premortal home to be tested and to gain experience. Our spirits needed to be clothed with physical bodies. We would need to leave our physical bodies at death and reunite with them in the Resurrection. Then we would receive immortal bodies like that of our

---

For teachers: Class members or family members are more likely to give a thoughtful answer to a question if they are given time to ponder their response. For example, after asking a question, you could say, "Please take a minute to think about your response, and then I'll ask for answers." Then give them time to ponder.

Heavenly Father. If we passed our tests, we would receive the fulness of joy that our Heavenly Father has received. (See D&C 93:30–34.)

Our Heavenly Father called a Grand Council to present His plan for our progression (see *Teachings of Presidents of the Church: Joseph Smith,* 209, 511). We learned that if we followed His plan, we would become like Him. We would be resurrected; we would have all power in heaven and on earth; we would become heavenly parents and have spirit children just as He does (see D&C 132:19–20).

We learned that He would provide an earth for us where we would prove ourselves (see Abraham 3:24–26). A veil would cover our memories, and we would forget our heavenly home. This would be necessary so we could exercise our agency to choose good or evil without being influenced by the memory of living with our Heavenly Father. Thus we could obey Him because of our faith in Him, not because of our knowledge or memory of Him. He would help us recognize the truth when we heard it again on earth (see John 18:37).

At the Grand Council we also learned the purpose for our progression: to have a fulness of joy. However, we also learned that some would be deceived, choose other paths, and lose their way. We learned that all of us would have trials in our lives: sickness, disappointment, pain, sorrow, and death. But we understood that these would be given to us for our experience and our good (see D&C 122:7). If we allowed them to, these trials would purify us rather than defeat us. They would teach us to have endurance, patience, and charity (see *Teachings of Presidents of the Church: Spencer W. Kimball* [2006], 15–16).

At this council we also learned that because of our weakness, all of us except little children would sin (see D&C 29:46–47). We learned that a Savior would be provided for us so we could overcome our sins and overcome death with resurrection. We learned that if we placed our faith in Him, obeying His word and following His example, we would be exalted and become like our Heavenly Father. We would receive a fulness of joy.

- List some of Heavenly Father's attributes. How does the plan of salvation help us develop these attributes?

Additional Scriptures

- Hebrews 12:9 (God is the Father of our spirits)
- Job 38:4–7 (premortal life implied)
- Abraham 3:22–28 (vision of premortal life)
- Jeremiah 1:5 (vision of premortal life)
- D&C 29:31–38 (vision of premortal life)
- Moses 3:4–7 (spiritual and temporal creations)
- 1 Corinthians 15:44 (spiritual and temporal creations)
- D&C 76:23–24 (begotten sons and daughters)
- D&C 132:11–26 (plan for progression)

Jesus Christ, Our Chosen Leader and Savior

Chapter 3

A Savior and Leader Was Needed

- Why did we need to leave Heavenly Father's presence? Why do we need a Savior?

When the plan for our salvation was presented to us in the premortal spirit world, we were so happy that we shouted for joy (see Job 38:7).

We understood that we would have to leave our heavenly home for a time. We would not live in the presence of our Heavenly Father. While we were away from Him, all of us would sin and some of us would lose our way. Our Heavenly Father knew and loved each one of us. He knew we would need help, so He planned a way to help us.

We needed a Savior to pay for our sins and teach us how to return to our Heavenly Father. Our Father said, "Whom shall I send?" (Abraham 3:27). Jesus Christ, who was called Jehovah, said, "Here am I, send me" (Abraham 3:27; see also Moses 4:1–4).

Jesus was willing to come to the earth, give His life for us, and take upon Himself our sins. He, like our Heavenly Father, wanted us to choose whether we would obey Heavenly Father's commandments. He knew we must be free to choose in order to prove ourselves worthy of exaltation. Jesus said, "Father, thy will be done, and the glory be thine forever" (Moses 4:2).

Satan, who was called Lucifer, also came, saying, "Behold, here am I, send me, I will be thy son, and I will redeem all mankind, that one soul shall not be lost, and surely I will do it; wherefore give me thine honor" (Moses 4:1). Satan wanted to force us all to do his

will. Under his plan, we would not be allowed to choose. He would take away the freedom of choice that our Father had given us. Satan wanted to have all the honor for our salvation. Under his proposal, our purpose in coming to earth would have been frustrated (see *Teachings of Presidents of the Church: David O. McKay* [2003], 207).

Jesus Christ Became Our Chosen Leader and Savior

- As you read this section, think about the feelings you have for the Savior.

After hearing both sons speak, Heavenly Father said, "I will send the first" (Abraham 3:27).

Jesus Christ was chosen and foreordained to be our Savior. Many scriptures tell about this (see, for example, 1 Peter 1:19–20; Moses 4:1–2). One scripture tells us that long before Jesus was born, He appeared to a Book of Mormon prophet known as the brother of Jared and said: "Behold, I am he who was prepared from the foundation of the world to redeem my people. Behold, I am Jesus Christ. . . . In me shall all mankind have life, and that eternally, even they who shall believe on my name" (Ether 3:14).

When Jesus lived on earth, He taught: "I came down from heaven, not to do mine own will, but the will of him that sent me. . . . And this is the will of him that sent me, that every one which seeth the Son, and believeth on him, may have everlasting life: and I will raise him up at the last day" (John 6:38, 40).

The War in Heaven

Because our Heavenly Father chose Jesus Christ to be our Savior, Satan became angry and rebelled. There was war in heaven. Satan and his followers fought against Jesus Christ and His followers. The Savior's followers "overcame [Satan] by the blood of the Lamb, and by the word of their testimony" (Revelation 12:11).

In this great rebellion, Satan and all the spirits who followed him were sent away from the presence of God and cast down from heaven. A third part of the hosts of heaven were punished for following Satan (see D&C 29:36). They were denied the right to receive mortal bodies.

Because we are here on earth and have mortal bodies, we know that we chose to follow Jesus Christ and our Heavenly Father. Satan and his followers are also on the earth, but as spirits. They have not forgotten who we are, and they are around us daily, tempting us and enticing us to do things that are not pleasing to our Heavenly Father. In our premortal life, we chose to follow Jesus Christ and accept God's plan. We must continue to follow Jesus Christ here on earth. Only by following Him can we return to our heavenly home.

- In what ways does the War in Heaven continue today?

We Have the Savior's Teachings to Follow

- Think about how the Savior's teachings have influenced you.

From the beginning, Jesus Christ has revealed the gospel, which tells us what we must do to return to our Heavenly Father. At the appointed time He came to earth Himself. He taught the plan of salvation and exaltation by His word and by the way He lived. He established His Church and His priesthood on the earth. He took our sins upon Himself.

By following His teachings, we can inherit a place in the celestial kingdom. He did His part to help us return to our heavenly home. It is now up to each of us to do our part and become worthy of exaltation.

Additional Scriptures

- Moses 4:1–4; Abraham 3:22–28 (Savior chosen in premortality)
- D&C 76:25–29 (War in Heaven)
- Revelation 12:7–9, 11 (Savior's followers in the War in Heaven overcame Satan by the blood of the Lamb and by the word of their testimony)
- Isaiah 14:12–15 (why Lucifer was cast out)

For teachers: You could have class members or family members study the "Additional Scriptures" as individuals, in pairs, or as an entire group.

Freedom to Choose

Chapter 4

Agency Is an Eternal Principle

- If someone asked you why it is important to have agency, what would you say?

"Thou mayest choose for thyself, for it is given unto thee" (Moses 3:17).

God has told us through His prophets that we are free to choose between good and evil. We may choose liberty and eternal life by following Jesus Christ. We are also free to choose captivity and death by following Satan. (See 2 Nephi 2:27.) The right to choose between good and evil and to act for ourselves is called agency.

In our premortal life we had moral agency. One purpose of earth life is to show what choices we will make (see 2 Nephi 2:15–16). If we were forced to choose the right, we would not be able to show what we would choose for ourselves. Also, we are happier doing things when we have made our own choices.

Agency was one of the principal issues to arise in the premortal Council in Heaven. It was one of the main causes of the conflict between the followers of Christ and the followers of Satan. Satan said, "Behold, here am I, send me, I will be thy son, and I will redeem all mankind, that one soul shall not be lost, and surely I will do it; wherefore give me thine honor" (Moses 4:1). In saying this, he "rebelled against [God] and sought to destroy the agency of man" (Moses 4:3). His offer was rejected, and he was cast out of heaven with his followers (see D&C 29:36–37).

Agency Is a Necessary Part of the Plan of Salvation

Agency makes our life on earth a period of testing. When planning the mortal creation of His children, God said, "We will prove

[test] them herewith, to see if they will do all things whatsoever the Lord their God shall command them" (Abraham 3:25). Without the gift of agency, we would have been unable to show our Heavenly Father whether we would do all that He commanded us. Because we are able to choose, we are responsible for our actions (see Helaman 14:30–31).

When we choose to live according to God's plan for us, our agency is strengthened. Right choices increase our power to make more right choices.

As we obey each of our Father's commandments, we grow in wisdom and strength of character. Our faith increases. We find it easier to make right choices.

We began to make choices as spirit children in our Heavenly Father's presence. Our choices there made us worthy to come to earth. Our Heavenly Father wants us to grow in faith, power, knowledge, wisdom, and all other good things. If we keep His commandments and make right choices, we will learn and understand. We will become like Him. (See D&C 93:28.)

- How does making right choices help us make more right choices?

Agency Requires That There Be a Choice

- Why is opposition necessary?

We cannot choose righteousness unless the opposites of good and evil are placed before us. Lehi, a great Book of Mormon prophet, told his son Jacob that in order to bring about the eternal purposes of God, there must be "an opposition in all things. If not so, . . . righteousness could not be brought to pass, neither wickedness, neither holiness nor misery, neither good nor bad" (2 Nephi 2:11).

God allows Satan to oppose the good. God said of Satan:

"I caused that he should be cast down;

"And he became Satan, yea, even the devil, the father of all lies, to deceive and to blind men, and to lead them captive at his will, even as many as would not hearken unto my voice" (Moses 4:3–4).

Satan does all he can to destroy God's work. He seeks "the misery of all mankind. . . . He seeketh that all men might be miserable like unto himself" (2 Nephi 2:18, 27). He does not love us. He does not want any good thing for us (see Moroni 7:17). He does not want us to be happy. He wants to make us his slaves. He uses many disguises to enslave us.

When we follow the temptations of Satan, we limit our choices. The following example suggests how this works. Imagine seeing a sign on the seashore that reads: "Danger—whirlpool. No swimming allowed here." We might think that is a restriction. But is it? We still have many choices. We are free to swim somewhere else. We are free to walk along the beach and pick up seashells. We are free to watch the sunset. We are free to go home. We are also free to ignore the sign and swim in the dangerous place. But once the whirlpool has us in its grasp and we are pulled under, we have very few choices. We can try to escape, or we can call for help, but we may drown.

Even though we are free to choose our course of action, we are not free to choose the consequences of our actions. The consequences, whether good or bad, follow as a natural result of any choice we make (see Galatians 6:7; Revelation 22:12).

Heavenly Father has told us how to escape the captivity of Satan. We must watch and pray always, asking God to help us withstand the temptations of Satan (see 3 Nephi 18:15). Our Heavenly Father will not allow us to be tempted beyond our power to resist (see 1 Corinthians 10:13; Alma 13:28).

God's commandments direct us away from danger and toward eternal life. By choosing wisely, we will gain exaltation, progress eternally, and enjoy perfect happiness (see 2 Nephi 2:27–28).

- What are some examples of actions that limit our choices? What are some examples of actions that give us more freedom?

For teachers: A simple picture can help learners focus their attention. If you discuss the analogy of a warning sign as it is presented in this chapter, you may want to draw a picture of such a sign on the board or on a large piece of paper.

Additional Scriptures

- Moses 7:32 (freedom of choice)
- Abraham 3:24–25 (earth life a test)
- Alma 41:3; Moroni 7:5–6 (works judged)
- 2 Nephi 2:11–16 (opposition is necessary)
- Moroni 7:12–17 (choosing good and evil)
- 2 Peter 2:19; John 8:34 (sin is bondage)
- 2 Nephi 2:28–29; Alma 40:12–13 (reward according to works)

The Creation

Chapter 5

God's Plan for Us

- Why did we need to come to the earth?

When we lived as spirit children with our heavenly parents, our Heavenly Father told us about His plan for us to become more like Him. We shouted for joy when we heard His plan (see Job 38:7). We were eager for new experiences. In order for these things to happen, we needed to leave our Father's presence and receive mortal bodies. We needed another place to live where we could prepare to become like Him. Our new home was called earth.

- Why do you think we shouted for joy when we learned of the plan of salvation?

Jesus Created the Earth

Jesus Christ created this world and everything in it. He also created many other worlds. He did so through the power of the priesthood, under the direction of our Heavenly Father. God the Father said, "Worlds without number have I created; . . . and by the Son I created them, which is mine Only Begotten" (Moses 1:33). We have other testimonies of this truth. Joseph Smith and Sidney Rigdon saw Jesus Christ in a vision. They testified "that by him, and through him, and of him, the worlds are and were created, and the inhabitants thereof are begotten sons and daughters unto God" (D&C 76:24).

Carrying Out the Creation

- What are the purposes of the Creation?

For teachers: Some class members or family members may not feel comfortable reading aloud. Before asking them to read aloud, you may want to ask, "Who would like to read?" Then call on individuals who have volunteered.

The earth and everything on it were created spiritually before they were created physically (see Moses 3:5). In planning to create the physical earth, Christ said to those who were with Him, "We will go down, for there is space there, . . . and we will make an earth whereon these [the spirit children of our Father in Heaven] may dwell" (Abraham 3:24).

Under the direction of the Father, Christ formed and organized the earth. He divided light from darkness to make day and night. He formed the sun, moon, and stars. He divided the waters from the dry land to make seas, rivers, and lakes. He made the earth beautiful and productive. He made grass, trees, flowers, and other plants of all kinds. These plants contained seeds from which new plants could grow. Then He created the animals—fish, cattle, insects, and birds of all kinds. These animals had the ability to reproduce their own kind.

Now the earth was ready for the greatest creation of all—mankind. Our spirits would be given bodies of flesh and blood so they could live on earth. "And I, God, said unto mine Only Begotten, which was with me from the beginning: Let us make man in our image, after our likeness; and it was so" (Moses 2:26). And so the first man, Adam, and the first woman, Eve, were formed and given bodies that resembled those of our heavenly parents. "In the image of God created he him; male and female created he them" (Genesis 1:27). When the Lord finished His creations, He was pleased and knew that His work was good, and He rested for a time.

God's Creations Show His Love

• How do God's creations show that He loves us?

We are now living in this beautiful world. Think of the sun, which gives us warmth and light. Think of the rain, which makes plants grow and makes the world feel clean and fresh. Think of how good it is to hear a bird singing or a friend laughing. Think of how wonderful our bodies are—how we can work and play and rest. When we consider all of these creations, we begin to understand what wise, powerful, and loving beings Jesus Christ and our Heavenly Father are. They have shown great love for us by providing for all of our needs.

Plant life and animal life were also made to give us joy. The Lord said, "Yea, all things which come of the earth, in the season thereof, are made for the benefit and the use of man, both to please the eye and to gladden the heart; yea, for food and for raiment, for taste and for smell, to strengthen the body and to enliven the soul" (D&C 59:18–19). Even though God's creations are many, He knows and loves them all. He said, "All things are numbered unto me, for they are mine and I know them" (Moses 1:35).

- What are some things you appreciate about God's creations?

Additional Scriptures

- Genesis 1; 2:1–7; Abraham 3:22–23; 4–5; Moses 1:27–42; 2–3 (accounts of the Creation)
- Hebrews 1:1–3; Colossians 1:12–17; D&C 38:1–3 (Jesus the Creator)
- D&C 59:18–20; Moses 2:26–31; D&C 104:13–17; Matthew 6:25–26 (Creation shows God's love)

The Fall of Adam and Eve

Chapter 6

Adam and Eve Were the First to Come to Earth

- What evidence helps us know that Adam and Eve were valiant spirits?

God prepared this earth as a home for His children. Adam and Eve were chosen to be the first people to live on the earth (see Moses 1:34; 4:26). Their part in our Father's plan was to bring mortality into the world. They were to be the first parents. (See D&C 107:54–56.)

Adam and Eve were among our Father's noblest children. In the spirit world Adam was called Michael the archangel (see D&C 27:11; Jude 1:9). He was chosen by our Heavenly Father to lead the righteous in the battle against Satan (see Revelation 12:7–9). Adam and Eve were foreordained to become our first parents. The Lord promised Adam great blessings: "I have set thee to be at the head; a multitude of nations shall come of thee, and thou art a prince over them forever" (D&C 107:55).

Eve was "the mother of all living" (Moses 4:26). God brought Adam and Eve together in marriage because "it was not good that the man should be alone" (Moses 3:18; see also 1 Corinthians 11:11). She shared Adam's responsibility and will also share his eternal blessings.

- What can we learn from the examples of Adam and Eve?

For teachers: Use questions at the beginning of a section to start a discussion and send class members or family members to the text to find more information. Use questions at the end of a section to help class members or family members ponder and discuss the meaning of what they have read and apply it in their lives.

The Garden of Eden

- Under what conditions did Adam and Eve live in the Garden of Eden?

When Adam and Eve were placed in the Garden of Eden, they were not yet mortal. In this state, "they would have had no children" (2 Nephi 2:23). There was no death. They had *physical* life because their spirits were housed in physical bodies made from the dust of the earth (see Moses 6:59; Abraham 5:7). They had *spiritual* life because they were in the presence of God. They had not yet made a choice between good and evil.

God commanded them to have children. He said, "Be fruitful, and multiply, and replenish the earth, and subdue it, and have dominion over . . . every living thing that moveth upon the earth" (Moses 2:28). God told them they could freely eat of every tree in the garden except one, the tree of knowledge of good and evil. Of that tree God said, "In the day thou eatest thereof thou shalt surely die" (Moses 3:17).

Satan, not knowing the mind of God but seeking to destroy God's plan, came to Eve in the Garden of Eden. He tempted her to eat of the fruit of the tree of knowledge of good and evil. He assured her that she and Adam would not die, but that they would "be as gods, knowing good and evil" (Moses 4:11). Eve yielded to the temptation and ate the fruit. When Adam learned what had happened, he chose to partake also. The changes that came upon Adam and Eve because they ate the fruit are called the Fall.

Adam and Eve's Separation from God

- What physical and spiritual changes occurred in Adam and Eve as a result of their transgression?

Because Adam and Eve had eaten the fruit of the tree of knowledge of good and evil, the Lord sent them out of the Garden of Eden into the world. Their physical condition changed as a result of their eating the forbidden fruit. As God had promised, they became mortal. They and their children would experience sickness, pain, and physical death.

Because of their transgression, Adam and Eve also suffered spiritual death. This meant they and their children could not walk and talk face to face with God. Adam and Eve and their children were separated from God both physically and spiritually.

Great Blessings Resulted from the Transgression

- How does the Fall provide opportunities for us to become like our Heavenly Father?

Some people believe Adam and Eve committed a serious sin when they ate of the tree of knowledge of good and evil. However, latter-day scriptures help us understand that their Fall was a necessary step in the plan of life and a great blessing to all of us. Because of the Fall, we are blessed with physical bodies, the right to choose between good and evil, and the opportunity to gain eternal life. None of these privileges would have been ours had Adam and Eve remained in the garden.

After the Fall, Eve said, "Were it not for our transgression we never should have had seed [children], and never should have known good and evil, and the joy of our redemption, and the eternal life which God giveth unto all the obedient" (Moses 5:11).

The prophet Lehi explained:

"And now, behold, if Adam had not transgressed he would not have fallen [been cut off from the presence of God], but he would have remained in the Garden of Eden. And all things which were created must have remained in the same state in which they were after they were created. . . .

"And they would have had no children; wherefore they would have remained in a state of innocence, having no joy, for they knew no misery; doing no good, for they knew no sin.

"But behold, all things have been done in the wisdom of him who knoweth all things.

"Adam fell that men might be; and men are, that they might have joy" (2 Nephi 2:22–25).

- Why do you think it is important to know about the Fall and how it influences us?

Additional Scriptures

- 1 Nephi 5:11; 2 Nephi 2:20 (Adam and Eve first parents, family)
- 2 Nephi 2:14–21 (opposition and the Fall; life a probation)
- 2 Nephi 2:22–26 (Fall part of the plan of salvation)

The Holy Ghost

Chapter 7

The Holy Ghost Came to Adam and Eve

• Why did Adam and Eve need the guidance of the Holy Ghost?

After Adam and Eve left the Garden of Eden, they began to till the earth and work at other tasks for their living. They had many children, and their sons and daughters also married and had children (see Moses 5:1–3). Thus, spirit children of our Heavenly Father began leaving His presence to come to the earth as they had been promised (see Abraham 3:24–25). As they came to earth, the memory of their heavenly home was taken from them. But our Father did not shut them away from His influence. He sent the Holy Ghost to comfort and help and guide all of His spirit children.

Adam and Eve called upon Heavenly Father in prayer. He spoke to them and gave them commandments, which they obeyed. An angel of the Lord came and taught Adam and Eve the plan of salvation. The Lord sent the Holy Ghost to testify of the Father and of the Son and to teach Adam and Eve the gospel. (See Moses 5:4–9.)

Through the power of the Holy Ghost, Adam "began to prophesy concerning all the families of the earth, saying: Blessed be the name of God, for because of my transgression my eyes are opened, and in this life I shall have joy, and again in the flesh I shall see God" (Moses 5:10). Because of the witness of the Holy Ghost to Eve, she said, "Were it not for our transgression we never should have had seed, and never should have known good and evil, and the joy of our redemption, and the eternal life which God giveth unto all the obedient" (Moses 5:11).

For teachers: When you call class members by their names, they know they are important to you and that you care about them. Learn their names, and call them by name during each lesson. Help them learn each other's names.

• How is our need for guidance from the Holy Ghost similar to that of Adam and Eve?

Attributes of the Holy Ghost

• How does the Holy Ghost differ from the Father and the Son? Why is that difference important to us?

The Holy Ghost is a member of the Godhead (see 1 John 5:7; D&C 20:28). He is a "personage of Spirit" (D&C 130:22). He can be in only one place at a time, but His influence can be everywhere at the same time.

Heavenly Father, Jesus Christ, and the Holy Ghost are called the Godhead. They are unified in purpose. Each has an important assignment in the plan of salvation. Our Heavenly Father is our Father and ruler. Jesus Christ is our Savior. The Holy Ghost is the revealer and testifier of all truth.

The Holy Ghost is our Heavenly Father's messenger and is a special gift to us (see chapter 21 in this book).

The Mission of the Holy Ghost

• What are some of the truths that the Holy Ghost reveals to us?

The mission of the Holy Ghost is to bear witness of the Father and the Son and of the truth of all things.

The Holy Ghost will witness to us that Jesus is our Savior and Redeemer (see 3 Nephi 28:11; D&C 20:27). He will reveal to us that our Heavenly Father is the Father of our spirits. He will help us understand that we can become exalted like our Heavenly Father. (See Romans 8:16–17.) The prophets of the Lord have promised, "By the power of the Holy Ghost ye may know the truth of all things" (Moroni 10:5).

Without the Holy Ghost, we could not know that Jesus is the Christ. The Apostle Paul wrote, "No man can say that Jesus is the Lord, but by the Holy Ghost" (1 Corinthians 12:3). The Savior Himself said, "And this is life eternal, that they might know thee the only true God, and Jesus Christ, whom thou hast sent" (John 17:3). It is by the power of the Holy Ghost that we are led to understand and live the gospel of Jesus Christ.

The convincing power of the Holy Ghost is so great that there can be no doubt that what He reveals to us is true. President Joseph Fielding Smith said:

"When a man has the manifestation from the Holy Ghost, it leaves an indelible impression on his soul, one that is not easily erased. It is Spirit speaking to spirit, and it comes with convincing force. A manifestation of an angel, or even of the Son of God himself, would impress the eye and mind, and eventually become dimmed, but the impressions of the Holy Ghost sink deeper into the soul and are more difficult to erase" (*Answers to Gospel Questions,* comp. Joseph Fielding Smith Jr., 5 vols. [1957–66], 2:151).

President Smith also said, "Through the Holy Ghost the truth is woven into the very fibre and sinews of the body so that it cannot be forgotten" (*Doctrines of Salvation,* comp. Bruce R. McConkie, 3 vols. [1954–56], 1:48).

As members of The Church of Jesus Christ of Latter-day Saints, we should make ourselves worthy to receive this special messenger and witness of our Heavenly Father and Jesus Christ.

- Think about times when the Holy Ghost has helped you grow in your testimony. As appropriate, share some of these experiences with class members or family members.

Additional Scriptures

- Moses 5 (story of Adam's family)
- D&C 130:22 (Holy Ghost identified)
- John 14:26; 15:26; 16:13; Luke 12:12; 2 Nephi 31:18; 32:5, 8; 33:1; Alma 14:11; 3 Nephi 27:20; 4 Nephi 1:48; Moroni 10:6–7; D&C 8:2–3; 11:12–13; 20:26 (roles of the Holy Ghost)

Praying to Our Heavenly Father

Chapter 8

What Is Prayer?

Jesus taught, "Ye must always pray unto the Father in my name" (3 Nephi 18:19).

Prayer is one of the greatest blessings we have while we are here on earth. Through prayer we can communicate with our Heavenly Father and seek His guidance daily.

Prayer is a sincere, heartfelt talk with our Heavenly Father. We should pray to God and to no one else. We do not pray to any other being or to anything made by man or God (see Exodus 20:3–5).

Why Do We Pray?

Prayer has been an important part of the gospel from the beginning of the world. An angel of the Lord commanded Adam and Eve to repent and call upon God in the name of the Son (see Moses 5:8). This commandment has never been taken away. Prayer will help us draw closer to God. All of our thoughts, our words, and our actions are influenced by our prayers.

We should pray for strength to resist the temptations of Satan and his followers (see 3 Nephi 18:15; D&C 10:5). We should pray to confess our sins to God and ask Him to forgive us (see Alma 38:14).

For teachers: This chapter is organized under five section headings. Each heading is a question about prayer. You could use these questions as a guide for your lesson. If the classroom setting allows for small group discussion, consider dividing class members into groups of two to four. Assign each group one of the sections in the chapter. Have each group read and discuss their assigned section and share personal experiences that relate to it. Then discuss the five sections as a class, focusing on the questions that are of most interest to class members.

"The Lord will never permit me or any other man who stands as President of this Church to lead you astray. It is not in the programme. It is not in the mind of God. If I were to attempt that, the Lord would remove me out of my place" (*Teachings of Presidents of the Church: Wilford Woodruff* [2004], 199).

• In what ways has the living prophet influenced the Church?

We Should Sustain the Lord's Prophet

• What can we do to follow and sustain the prophet?

Many people find it easy to believe in the prophets of the past. But it is much greater to believe in and follow the living prophet. We raise our hands to sustain the President of the Church as prophet, seer, and revelator.

How can we sustain the prophet? We should pray for him. His burdens are heavy, and he needs to be strengthened by the prayers of the Saints.

We should study his words. We can listen to his conference addresses. We can also subscribe to the *Ensign* or *Liahona* so we can read his conference addresses and other messages he gives.

We should follow his inspired teachings completely. We should not choose to follow part of his inspired counsel and discard that which is unpleasant or difficult. The Lord commanded us to follow the inspired teachings of His prophet:

"Thou shalt give heed unto all his [the prophet's] words and commandments which he shall give unto you as he receiveth them, walking in all holiness before me;

"For his word ye shall receive, as if from mine own mouth, in all patience and faith" (D&C 21:4–5).

The Lord will never allow the President of the Church to lead us astray.

• What has the President of the Church taught or emphasized recently?

Great Blessings Follow Obedience to the Prophet

If we obey, the Lord promises, "The gates of hell shall not prevail against you; yea, and the Lord God will disperse the powers of darkness from before you, and cause the heavens to shake for your good, and his name's glory" (D&C 21:6). When we do as our prophet directs, blessings pour down from heaven.

In order to stand, the true Church must be "built upon the foundation of the apostles and prophets, Jesus Christ himself being the chief corner stone" (Ephesians 2:20). We are blessed in this insecure world to have a prophet through whom the Lord reveals His will.

- What experiences have you had when you have obeyed the counsel of the prophet?

Additional Scriptures

- Numbers 12:6 (God speaks through prophets)
- 1 Samuel 9:9 (prophet called a seer)
- Amos 3:7 (God reveals His secrets to the prophets)
- Mosiah 8:16–18 (a seer can know of things past and things to come)
- Luke 1:70 (God speaks through prophets)
- D&C 45:10, 15 (God speaks today as in days of old)
- 1 Nephi 22:2 (by the Spirit things are made known to prophets)
- D&C 68:3–5 (when the Lord's servants speak as moved by the Holy Ghost, it is the mind, will, and voice of the Lord)
- D&C 107:65–67, 91–92 (duties of the President of the Church)
- D&C 43:1–7 (only the prophet is authorized to receive revelations for the Church)

For teachers: Sharing experiences and bearing testimony invite the Spirit. As you conclude this lesson, consider sharing an experience you have had when you have followed the counsel of the President of the Church. Share your testimony of the living prophet.

Scriptures

Chapter 10

The Scriptures Are Available to Us Today

- What are some of the blessings that we enjoy today because the scriptures are so accessible?

When the Lord's servants speak or write under the influence of the Holy Ghost, their words become scripture (see D&C 68:4). From the beginning, the Lord has commanded His prophets to keep a record of His revelations and His dealings with His children. He said: "I command all men, both in the east and in the west, and in the north, and in the south, and in the islands of the sea, that they shall write the words which I speak unto them; for out of the books which shall be written I will judge the world, every man according to their works, according to that which is written" (2 Nephi 29:11).

The Church of Jesus Christ of Latter-day Saints accepts four books as scripture: the Bible, the Book of Mormon, the Doctrine and Covenants, and the Pearl of Great Price. These books are called the standard works of the Church. The inspired words of our living prophets are also accepted as scripture.

The Bible

The Bible is a collection of sacred writings containing God's revelations to man. These writings cover many centuries, from the time of Adam through the time when the Apostles of Jesus Christ lived. They were written by many prophets who lived at various times in the history of the world.

For teachers: To encourage discussion about the four standard works, you could assign each class member or family member a number between 1 and 4. Ask those with number 1 to read what this chapter teaches about the Bible, those with number 2 to read what this chapter teaches about the Book of Mormon, those with number 3 to read what this chapter teaches about the Doctrine and Covenants, and those with number 4 to read what this chapter teaches about the Pearl of Great Price. Then ask them to share what they have learned.

The Bible is divided into two sections: the Old Testament and the New Testament. Many prophecies in the Old Testament foretell the coming of a Savior and Redeemer. The New Testament tells of the life of that Savior and Redeemer, who is Jesus Christ. It also tells of the establishing of His Church in that day. "We believe the Bible to be the word of God as far as it is translated correctly" (Articles of Faith 1:8).

Through the Prophet Joseph Smith, the Lord has expanded our understanding of some passages in the Bible. The Lord inspired the Prophet Joseph to restore truths to the Bible text that had been lost or changed since the original words were written. These inspired corrections are called the Joseph Smith Translation of the Bible. In the Latter-day Saint edition of the King James Version of the Bible, selected passages from the Joseph Smith Translation are found on pages 797–813 and in many footnotes.

The Book of Mormon

The Book of Mormon is a sacred record of some of the people who lived on the American continents between about 2000 B.C. and A.D. 400. It contains the fulness of the gospel of Jesus Christ (see D&C 20:9; 42:12; 135:3). The Book of Mormon tells of the visit Jesus Christ made to the people in the Americas soon after His Resurrection.

Joseph Smith translated the Book of Mormon into English through the gift and power of God. He said that it is "the most correct of any book on earth, and the keystone of our religion, and a man would get nearer to God by abiding by its precepts, than by any other book" (introduction to the Book of Mormon).

President Ezra Taft Benson helped us understand how the Book of Mormon is the keystone of our religion. He said:

"There are three ways in which the Book of Mormon is the keystone of our religion. It is the keystone in our witness of Christ. It is the keystone of our doctrine. It is the keystone of testimony.

"The Book of Mormon is the keystone in our witness of Jesus Christ, who is Himself the cornerstone of everything we do. It bears witness of His reality with power and clarity. . . .

"[It] broadens our understandings of the doctrines of salvation. . . . The Book of Mormon . . . was written for our day. . . . In [it] we find a pattern for preparing for the Second Coming. . . .

". . . The Book of Mormon teaches us truth [and] bears testimony of Christ. . . . But there is something more. There is a power in the book which will begin to flow into your lives the moment you begin a serious study of the book. You will find greater power to resist temptation. You will find the power to avoid deception. You will find the power to stay on the strait and narrow path. The scriptures are called 'the words of life,' and nowhere is that more true than it is of the Book of Mormon. . . . 'Every Latter-day Saint should make the study of this book a lifetime pursuit' " (in Conference Report, Oct. 1986, 4–7; or *Ensign,* Nov. 1986, 5–7; quoting Marion G. Romney, in Conference Report, Apr. 1980, 90; or *Ensign,* May 1980, 67).

The Doctrine and Covenants

The Doctrine and Covenants is a collection of modern revelations. In section 1 of the Doctrine and Covenants, the Lord reveals that the book is published to the inhabitants of the earth to prepare them for His coming:

"Wherefore the voice of the Lord is unto the ends of the earth, that all that will hear may hear:

"Prepare ye, prepare ye for that which is to come, for the Lord is nigh" (D&C 1:11–12).

This book contains the revelations regarding the Church of Jesus Christ as it has been restored in these last days. Several sections of the book explain the organization of the Church and define the offices of the priesthood and their functions. Other sections, such as sections 76 and 88, contain glorious truths that were lost to the world for hundreds of years. Still others, such as sections 29 and 93, shed light on teachings in the Bible. In addition, some sections, such as section 133, contain prophecies of events to come. God has commanded us to study His revelations in this book: "Search these commandments, for they are true and faithful, and the prophecies and promises which are in them shall all be fulfilled" (D&C 1:37).

The Pearl of Great Price

The Pearl of Great Price contains the book of Moses, the book of Abraham, and some inspired writings of Joseph Smith. The book of Moses contains an account of some of the visions and writings of Moses, revealed to the Prophet Joseph Smith. It clarifies doctrines and teachings that were lost from the Bible and gives added information concerning the Creation of the earth.

The book of Abraham was translated by the Prophet Joseph Smith from a papyrus scroll taken from the Egyptian catacombs. This book contains valuable information about the Creation, the gospel, the nature of God, and the priesthood.

The writings of Joseph Smith include part of Joseph Smith's inspired translation of the Bible, selections from his *History of the Church,* and the Articles of Faith.

- What are some stories from the scriptures that have inspired you? What are some teachings from these books of scripture that have helped you?

Words of Our Living Prophets

In addition to these four books of scripture, the inspired words of our living prophets become scripture to us. Their words come to us through conferences, the *Liahona* or *Ensign* magazine, and instructions to local priesthood leaders. "We believe all that God has revealed, all that He does now reveal, and we believe that He will yet reveal many great and important things pertaining to the Kingdom of God" (Articles of Faith 1:9).

- Where can we find the words of our living prophets?

Studying the Scriptures

- What blessings can we receive when we study the scriptures?

We should each study the scriptures every day. We should share these truths with our children. We should read the standard works with our children so they will learn to love them and use them for the truths they contain.

If we desire to avoid the evils of this world, we must feed our minds with the truth and righteousness found in the scriptures. We will grow closer to God and to each other as we read and ponder the scriptures together.

As we read, ponder, and pray about the scriptures and ask God for understanding, the Holy Ghost will bear witness to us of the truth of these things. We will each know for ourselves that these things are true. We will not be deceived (see Joseph Smith—Matthew 1:37). We can receive the same feelings Nephi expressed when he said, "My soul delighteth in the things of the Lord; and my heart pondereth continually upon the things which I have seen and heard" (2 Nephi 4:16).

- How can we keep the commitment to study the scriptures each day? Consider planning a time and a place to study the scriptures each day.

Additional Scriptures

- 1 Nephi 14:20–26 (prophets commanded to write)
- 1 Nephi 19:1–3, 6–7; Alma 37:1–8 (great worth of scriptures)
- 2 Nephi 33:10 (scriptures testify of Christ)
- Alma 29:8 (Lord speaks to all nations through scriptures)
- Alma 31:5; Helaman 3:29–30 (the word of God is powerful)
- Helaman 15:7–8 (scriptures lead us to be firm and steadfast in the faith)
- 2 Timothy 3:16–17; 1 Nephi 19:21–24 (why and how scriptures are given)
- 2 Peter 1:20; Alma 13:20; D&C 10:62 (scriptures bring to light true points of doctrine)
- D&C 128:18; Articles of Faith 1:9; 1 Nephi 14:25–26 (scriptures yet to come)
- 2 Nephi 29:3–10 (scriptures to Jews and to Gentiles)

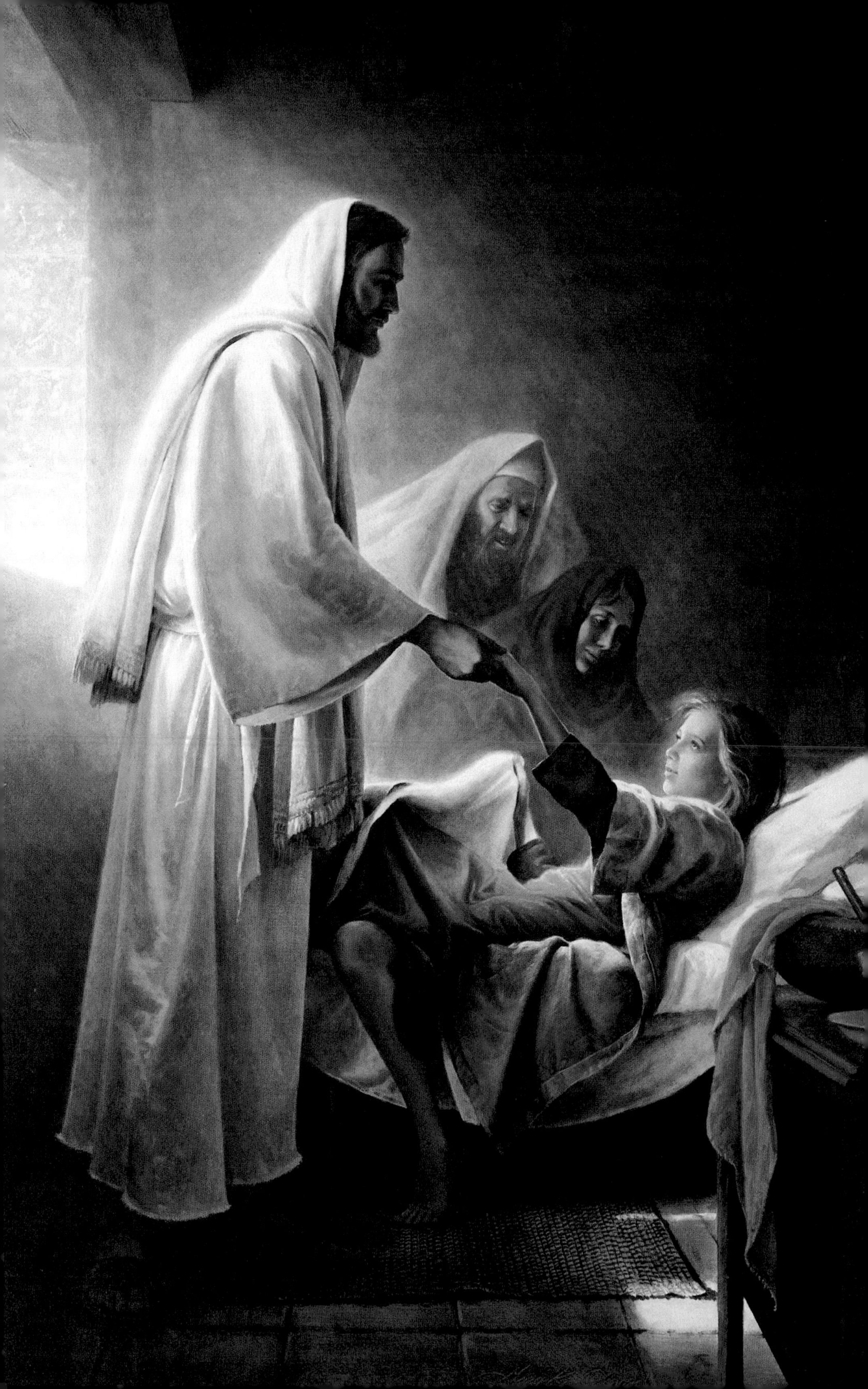

The Life of Christ

Chapter 11

The Life of Christ Was Predicted Long before His Birth

Every person who comes to earth depends on Jesus Christ to fulfill the promise He made in heaven to be our Savior. Without Him, the plan of salvation would have failed. Because His mission was necessary, all of the prophets from Adam to Christ testified that He would come (see Acts 10:43). All of the prophets since Christ have testified that He did come. All of us need to study the life of the Savior and follow Him faithfully throughout our lives.

Adam learned that the Savior's name would be Jesus Christ (see Moses 6:51–52). Enoch saw that Jesus would die upon the cross and be resurrected (see Moses 7:55–56). Noah and Moses also testified of Him (see Moses 1:11; 8:23–24). About 800 years before the Savior was born on the earth, Isaiah foresaw His life. When Isaiah saw the grief and sorrow that the Savior would suffer to pay the price for our sins, he exclaimed:

"He is despised and rejected of men; a man of sorrows, and acquainted with grief. . . .

". . . Surely he hath borne our griefs, and carried our sorrows. . . .

"He was wounded for our transgressions, he was bruised for our iniquities. . . .

"He was oppressed, and he was afflicted, yet he opened not his mouth: he is brought as a lamb to the slaughter" (Isaiah 53:3–5, 7).

Nephi also saw a vision of the Savior's future birth and mission. He saw a beautiful virgin, and an angel explained, "Behold, the virgin whom thou seest is the mother of the Son of God, after the manner

For teachers: This chapter probably has more material than you will be able to cover in class. As you study it in preparation to teach, seek the Spirit's guidance in determining which portions will be most helpful for those you teach.

of the flesh" (1 Nephi 11:18). Then Nephi saw the virgin holding a child in her arms. The angel declared, "Behold the Lamb of God, yea, even the Son of the Eternal Father!" (1 Nephi 11:21).

About 124 years before Jesus was born, King Benjamin, another Nephite prophet, also foresaw the Savior's life:

"For behold, the time cometh, and is not far distant, that with power, the Lord Omnipotent who reigneth, who was, and is from all eternity to all eternity, shall come down from heaven among the children of men, and shall dwell in a tabernacle of clay, and shall go forth amongst men, working mighty miracles, such as healing the sick, raising the dead, causing the lame to walk, the blind to receive their sight, and the deaf to hear, and curing all manner of diseases.

"And he shall cast out devils, or the evil spirits which dwell in the hearts of the children of men.

"And lo, he shall suffer temptations, and pain of body, hunger, thirst, and fatigue, even more than man can suffer, except it be unto death; for behold, blood cometh from every pore, so great shall be his anguish for the wickedness and the abominations of his people.

"And he shall be called Jesus Christ, the Son of God, the Father of heaven and earth, the Creator of all things from the beginning; and his mother shall be called Mary" (Mosiah 3:5–8).

- What are some ancient prophecies about Jesus Christ?

He Was the Only Begotten of the Father

- What did Jesus Christ inherit from His Father? What did He inherit from His mother?

The story of the birth and life of the Savior is found in the New Testament in the books of Matthew, Mark, Luke, and John. From their accounts we learn that Jesus was born of a virgin named Mary. She was engaged to marry Joseph when an angel of the Lord appeared to her. The angel told her that she was to be the mother of the Son of God. She asked him how this was possible (see Luke 1:34). He told her, "The Holy Ghost shall come upon thee, and the power of the Highest shall overshadow thee: therefore also that holy thing which shall be born of thee shall be called the Son of God" (Luke 1:35). Thus, God the Father became the literal Father of Jesus Christ.

Jesus is the only person on earth to be born of a mortal mother and an immortal Father. That is why He is called the Only Begotten Son. He inherited divine powers from His Father. From His mother He inherited mortality and was subject to hunger, thirst, fatigue, pain, and death. No one could take the Savior's life from Him unless He willed it. He had power to lay it down and power to take up His body again after dying. (See John 10:17–18.)

He Led a Perfect Life

• What does the Savior's life mean for us?

From His youth, Jesus obeyed all that was required of Him by our Heavenly Father. Under the guidance of Mary and Joseph, Jesus grew much as other children grow. He loved and obeyed the truth. Luke tells us, "And the child grew, and waxed strong in spirit, filled with wisdom: and the grace of God was upon him" (Luke 2:40; see also D&C 93:12–14).

By the time He was 12 years old, Jesus had grown in His understanding that He had been sent to do the will of His Father. He went with His parents to Jerusalem. When His parents were returning home, they discovered that He was not with their group. They went back to Jerusalem to look for Him. "After three days they found him in the temple, sitting in the midst of the doctors, and they were hearing him, and asking him questions" (Joseph Smith Translation, Luke 2:46). "And all that heard him were astonished at his understanding and answers" (Luke 2:47).

Joseph and Mary were relieved to find Him, but "they were amazed: and his mother said unto him, Son, why hast thou thus dealt with us? behold, thy father and I have sought thee sorrowing." Jesus answered her, saying, "Wist ye not that I must be about my [Heavenly] Father's business?" (Luke 2:48–49).

In order to fulfill His mission, Jesus was to do the will of His Father in Heaven. "I do nothing of myself," He declared, "but as my Father hath taught me, I speak these things. . . . I do always those things that please him" (John 8:28–29).

When Jesus was 30 years old, He came to John the Baptist to be baptized in the Jordan River. John was reluctant to baptize Jesus because he knew that Jesus was greater than he. Jesus asked John to baptize Him in order "to fulfil all righteousness." John did baptize the Savior, immersing Him completely in the water. When Jesus was baptized, His Father spoke from heaven, saying, "This is my beloved Son, in whom I am well pleased." The Holy Ghost descended, as shown by the sign of the dove. (See Matthew 3:13–17.)

Soon after Jesus was baptized, He fasted for 40 days and 40 nights to be with God. After that, Satan came to tempt Him. Jesus firmly resisted all of Satan's temptations and then commanded Satan to leave. (See Matthew 4:1–11; see also Joseph Smith Translation, Matthew 4:1, 5–6, 8–9, 11.) Jesus Christ remained sinless, the one perfect being to ever walk the earth (see Hebrews 4:15; 1 Peter 2:21–22).

- Which accounts from the Savior's life are especially meaningful to you?

He Taught Us How to Love and Serve One Another

- How did the Savior teach us how to love and serve one another?

After His fast and His encounter with Satan, Jesus began His public ministry. He came to earth not only to die for us but also to teach us how to live. He taught that there are two great commandments: first, to love God with all our heart, mind, and strength; and second, to love others as we love ourselves (see Matthew 22:36–39). His life is an example of how we should obey these two commandments. If we love God, we will trust and obey Him, as Jesus did. If we love others, we will help them meet their physical and spiritual needs.

Jesus spent His life serving others. He cured them of diseases. He made the blind see, the deaf hear, and the lame walk. Once when He was healing the sick, it became late and the people were hungry. Instead of sending them away, He blessed five loaves of bread and two fishes and miraculously was able to feed a multitude of 5,000 people. (See Matthew 14:14–21.) He taught that whenever we find people hungry, cold, naked, or lonely, we should help them all we can. When we help others, we are serving the Lord. (See Matthew 25:35–46.)

Jesus loved others with all His heart. Often His heart was so full of compassion that He wept. He loved little children, the elderly, and the humble, simple people who had faith in Him. He loved those who had sinned, and with great compassion He taught them to repent and be baptized. He taught, "I am the way, the truth, and the life" (John 14:6).

Jesus even loved those who sinned against him and were unrepentant. At the end of His life, as He hung on the cross, He prayed to the Father for the soldiers who had crucified Him, pleading, "Father, forgive them; for they know not what they do" (Luke 23:34). He taught, "This is my commandment, That ye love one another, as I have loved you" (John 15:12).

- In what ways can we show the Lord that we love Him?

He Organized the Only True Church

- Why did the Savior organize His Church and ordain Apostles?

Jesus wanted His gospel taught to people all over the earth, so He chose twelve Apostles to testify of Him. They were the original leaders of His Church. They received the authority to act in His name and do the works they had seen Him do. Those who received authority from them were also able to teach, baptize, and perform other ordinances in His name. After His death, they continued to do His work until the people became so wicked that they killed the Apostles.

He Redeemed Us from Our Sins and Saved Us from Death

- As you study this section, take time to ponder the events of the Atonement.

Near the end of His mortal ministry, Jesus prepared to make the ultimate sacrifice for all the sins of mankind. He had been

For teachers: Pondering invites the Spirit. Consider asking class members or family members to quietly read the final two sections of the chapter, thinking about their feelings for the Savior. Then invite those who feel comfortable doing so to share their thoughts with the class.

condemned to die because He had testified to the people that He was the Son of God.

The night before His Crucifixion, Jesus went to a garden called Gethsemane. Soon He was weighed down by deep sorrow and wept as He prayed. Latter-day Apostle Orson F. Whitney was permitted to see the Savior's suffering in a vision. Seeing the Savior weep, he said: "I was so moved at the sight that I also wept, out of pure sympathy. My whole heart went out to Him; I loved Him with all my soul, and longed to be with Him as I longed for nothing else" ("The Divinity of Jesus Christ," *Improvement Era,* Jan. 1926, 224–25; see also *Ensign,* Dec. 2003, 10). Jesus "went a little further, and fell on his face, and prayed, saying, O my Father, if it be possible, let this cup pass from me: nevertheless not as I will, but as thou wilt" (Matthew 26:39).

In a modern revelation the Savior described how great His suffering was, saying it caused Him "to tremble because of pain, and to bleed at every pore, and to suffer both body and spirit" (D&C 19:18). He suffered "according to the flesh," taking upon himself our pains, sicknesses, infirmities, and sins (see Alma 7:10–13). No mortal person can comprehend just how great this burden was. No other person could have endured such agony of body and spirit. "He descended below all things . . . that he might be in all and through all things, the light of truth" (D&C 88:6).

But His suffering was not yet complete. The following day, Jesus was beaten, humiliated, and spit upon. He was required to carry His own cross; then He was lifted up and nailed to it. He was tortured in one of the cruelest ways men have ever devised. After suffering on the cross, He cried out in agony, "My God, my God, why hast thou forsaken me?" (Mark 15:34). In Jesus's bitterest hour, the Father had withdrawn from Him so Jesus could finish suffering the penalty for the sins of all mankind that Jesus might have complete victory over the forces of sin and death (see James E. Talmage, *Jesus the Christ,* 3rd ed. [1916], 660–61).

When the Savior knew that His sacrifice had been accepted by the Father, He exclaimed in a loud voice, "It is finished" (John 19:30).

"Father, into thy hands I commend my spirit" (Luke 23:46). He bowed His head and voluntarily gave up His spirit. The Savior was dead. A violent earthquake shook the earth.

Some friends took the Savior's body to a tomb, where it lay until the third day. During this time His spirit went and organized the missionary work to other spirits who needed to receive His gospel (see 1 Peter 3:18–20; D&C 138). On the third day, a Sunday, He returned to His body and took it up again. He was the first to overcome death. The prophecy had been fulfilled "that he must rise again from the dead" (John 20:9).

Shortly after His Resurrection, the Savior appeared to the Nephites and established His Church in the Americas. He taught the people and blessed them. This moving account is found in 3 Nephi 11 through 28.

His Sacrifice Showed His Love for His Father and for Us

Jesus taught: "Greater love hath no man than this, that a man lay down his life for his friends. Ye are my friends, if ye do whatsoever I command you" (John 15:13–14). He willingly and humbly went through the sorrow in Gethsemane and the suffering on the cross so we could receive all the blessings of the plan of salvation. To receive these blessings, we must come unto Him, repent of our sins, and love Him with all our hearts. He said:

"And this is the gospel which I have given unto you—that I came into the world to do the will of my Father, because my Father sent me.

"And my Father sent me that I might be lifted up upon the cross; and after that I had been lifted up upon the cross, that I might draw all men unto me . . . that they may be judged according to their works. . . .

"For the works which ye have seen me do that shall ye also do. . . .

"Therefore, what manner of men ought ye to be? Verily I say unto you, *even as I am*" (3 Nephi 27:13–15, 21, 27; italics added).

- What are your feelings as you ponder the Savior's sacrifice for you?

Additional Scriptures and Other Sources

- 2 Nephi 25:12 (the Only Begotten of the Father in the flesh)
- Moses 6:57 (Jesus Christ named as the Only Begotten)
- Matthew, Mark, Luke, John (life and teachings of Jesus Christ)
- Matthew 10:1–8; Luke 9:1–2 (Apostles ordained with power and authority)
- Matthew 26–28; Mark 14–16; Luke 22–24; John 18–20 (Jesus in the garden; betrayed, crucified, and resurrected)
- "The Living Christ: The Testimony of the Apostles," *Ensign,* Apr. 2000, 2–3

The Atonement

Chapter 12

The Atonement Is Necessary for Our Salvation

• Why is the Atonement necessary for our salvation?

Jesus Christ "came into the world . . . to be crucified for the world, and to bear the sins of the world, and to sanctify the world, and to cleanse it from all unrighteousness; that through him all might be saved" (D&C 76:41–42). The great sacrifice He made to pay for our sins and overcome death is called the Atonement. It is the most important event that has ever occurred in the history of mankind: "For it is expedient that an atonement should be made; for according to the great plan of the Eternal God there must be an atonement made, or else all mankind must unavoidably perish; . . . yea, all are fallen and are lost, and must perish except it be through the atonement" (Alma 34:9).

The Fall of Adam brought two kinds of death into the world: physical death and spiritual death. Physical death is separation of the body and spirit. Spiritual death is separation from God. If these two kinds of death had not been overcome by Jesus Christ's Atonement, two consequences would have resulted: our bodies and our spirits would have been separated forever, and we could not have lived again with our Heavenly Father (see 2 Nephi 9:7–9).

But our wise Heavenly Father prepared a wonderful, merciful plan to save us from physical and spiritual death. He planned for a Savior to come to earth to ransom (redeem) us from our sins and from death. Because of our sins and the weakness of our mortal bodies, we could not ransom ourselves (see Alma 34:10–12). The one who would be our Savior would need to be sinless and to have power over death.

For teachers: Simple charts and pictures can help class members or family members understand principles and doctrines. Consider making a chart with two columns, one labeled *Results of the Fall* and the other labeled *Blessings of the Atonement.* Use information from this chapter to fill in the chart.

Jesus Christ Was the Only One Who Could Atone for Our Sins

• Why was Jesus Christ the only one who could atone for our sins?

There are several reasons why Jesus Christ was the only person who could be our Savior. One reason is that Heavenly Father chose Him to be the Savior. He was the Only Begotten Son of God and thus had power over death. Jesus explained: "I lay down my life, that I might take it again. No man taketh it from me, but I lay it down of myself. I have power to lay it down, and I have power to take it again" (John 10:17–18).

Jesus also qualified to be our Savior because He is the only person who has ever lived on the earth who did not sin. This made Him a worthy sacrifice to pay for the sins of others.

Christ Suffered and Died to Atone for Our Sins

• As you read this section, imagine yourself in the Garden of Gethsemane or at the cross as a witness of the suffering of Jesus Christ.

The Savior atoned for our sins by suffering in Gethsemane and by giving His life on the cross. It is impossible for us to fully understand how He suffered for all of our sins. In the Garden of Gethsemane, the weight of our sins caused Him to feel such agony that He bled from every pore (see D&C 19:18–19). Later, as He hung upon the cross, Jesus suffered painful death by one of the most cruel methods known to man.

How Jesus loves us, to suffer such spiritual and physical agony for our sake! How great the love of Heavenly Father that He would send His Only Begotten Son to suffer and die for the rest of His children. "For God so loved the world, that he gave his only begotten Son, that whosoever believeth in him should not perish, but have everlasting life" (John 3:16).

The Atonement and Resurrection Bring Resurrection to All

On the third day after His Crucifixion, Christ took up His body again and became the first person to be resurrected. When His friends went to seek Him, the angels who guarded His tomb told

"The creditor replied, 'Mercy is always so one-sided. It would serve only you. If I show mercy to you, it will leave me unpaid. It is justice I demand. Do you believe in justice?'

" 'I believed in justice when I signed the contract,' the debtor said. 'It was on my side then, for I thought it would protect me. I did not need mercy then, nor think I should need it ever. Justice, I thought, would serve both of us equally as well.'

" 'It is justice that demands that you pay the contract or suffer the penalty,' the creditor replied. 'That is the law. You have agreed to it and that is the way it must be. Mercy cannot rob justice.'

"There they were: One meting out justice, the other pleading for mercy. Neither could prevail except at the expense of the other.

" 'If you do not forgive the debt there will be no mercy,' the debtor pleaded.

" 'If I do, there will be no justice,' was the reply.

"Both laws, it seemed, could not be served. They are two eternal ideals that appear to contradict one another. Is there no way for justice to be fully served, and mercy also?

"There is a way! The law of justice *can* be fully satisfied and mercy *can* be fully extended—but it takes someone else. And so it happened this time.

"The debtor had a friend. He came to help. He knew the debtor well. He knew him to be shortsighted. He thought him foolish to have gotten himself into such a predicament. Nevertheless, he wanted to help because he loved him. He stepped between them, faced the creditor, and made this offer.

" 'I will pay the debt if you will free the debtor from his contract so that he may keep his possessions and not go to prison.'

"As the creditor was pondering the offer, the mediator added, 'You demanded justice. Though he cannot pay you, I will do so. You will have been justly dealt with and can ask no more. It would not be just.'

"And so the creditor agreed.

"The mediator turned then to the debtor. 'If I pay your debt, will you accept me as your creditor?'

" 'Oh yes, yes,' cried the debtor. 'You save me from prison and show mercy to me.'

" 'Then,' said the benefactor, 'you will pay the debt to me and I will set the terms. It will not be easy, but it will be possible. I will provide a way. You need not go to prison.'

"And so it was that the creditor was paid in full. He had been justly dealt with. No contract had been broken.

"The debtor, in turn, had been extended mercy. Both laws stood fulfilled. Because there was a mediator, justice had claimed its full share, and mercy was fully satisfied" (in Conference Report, Apr. 1977, 79–80; or *Ensign,* May 1977, 54–55).

Our sins are our spiritual debts. Without Jesus Christ, who is our Savior and Mediator, we would all pay for our sins by suffering spiritual death. But because of Him, if we will keep His terms, which are to repent and keep His commandments, we may return to live with our Heavenly Father.

It is wonderful that Christ has provided us a way to be healed from our sins. He said:

"Behold, I have come unto the world . . . to save the world from sin.

"Therefore, whoso repenteth and cometh unto me as a little child, him will I receive, for of such is the kingdom of God. Behold, for such I have laid down my life, and have taken it up again; therefore repent, and come unto me ye ends of the earth, and be saved" (3 Nephi 9:21–22).

- Ponder how you can show gratitude for the gift of the Atonement.

Additional Scriptures

- Alma 34:9–16 (Atonement necessary; sacrifice of God)
- 2 Nephi 9:7–12 (the Atonement saves us from physical and spiritual death)
- Romans 5:12–17 (by one came death, by one came life)

- Helaman 14:15–18 (purpose of Jesus's death)
- Articles of Faith 1:3 (all may be saved)
- 1 Peter 1:18–20 (Jesus was foreordained)
- Matthew 16:21 (Jesus's sacrifice was necessary)
- Luke 22:39–46 (Jesus's suffering in the garden)
- 1 John 1:7 (Jesus cleanses from sin)
- 2 Nephi 9:21–22 (the Savior suffered for all people)
- Mosiah 16:6–8 (resurrection possible only through Jesus)
- Alma 11:40–45; Mormon 9:12–14 (all to be resurrected)
- Isaiah 1:18 (sins shall be made white)
- 1 Corinthians 15:40–44; Alma 40:23 (description of the Resurrection)

The Priesthood

Chapter 13

What Is the Priesthood?

The priesthood is the eternal power and authority of God. Through the priesthood He created and governs the heavens and the earth. By this power the universe is kept in perfect order. Through this power He accomplishes His work and glory, which is "to bring to pass the immortality and eternal life of man" (Moses 1:39).

Our Heavenly Father delegates His priesthood power to worthy male members of the Church. The priesthood enables them to act in God's name for the salvation of the human family. Through it they can be authorized to preach the gospel, administer the ordinances of salvation, and govern God's kingdom on earth.

- Think about the significance of God allowing worthy men and boys to hold His priesthood.

Why Do We Need the Priesthood on the Earth?

We must have priesthood authority to act in the name of God when performing the sacred ordinances of the gospel, such as baptism, confirmation, administration of the sacrament, and temple marriage. If a man does not have the priesthood, even though he may be sincere, the Lord will not recognize ordinances he performs (see Matthew 7:21–23; Articles of Faith 1:5). These important ordinances must be performed on the earth by men holding the priesthood.

For teachers: This chapter is organized under five headings. Each heading is a question about the priesthood. You could use these questions as a guide for your lesson. If the classroom setup allows for small group discussion, consider dividing class members into groups of two to four. Assign each group one of the sections of the chapter (in large classes, some sections may be assigned to more than one group). Have each group do the following: (1) Read and discuss their assigned section. (2) Find scriptures that help answer the question in the section heading. (3) Share personal experiences that relate to the section. Then ask class members to share some of these experiences with the entire class.

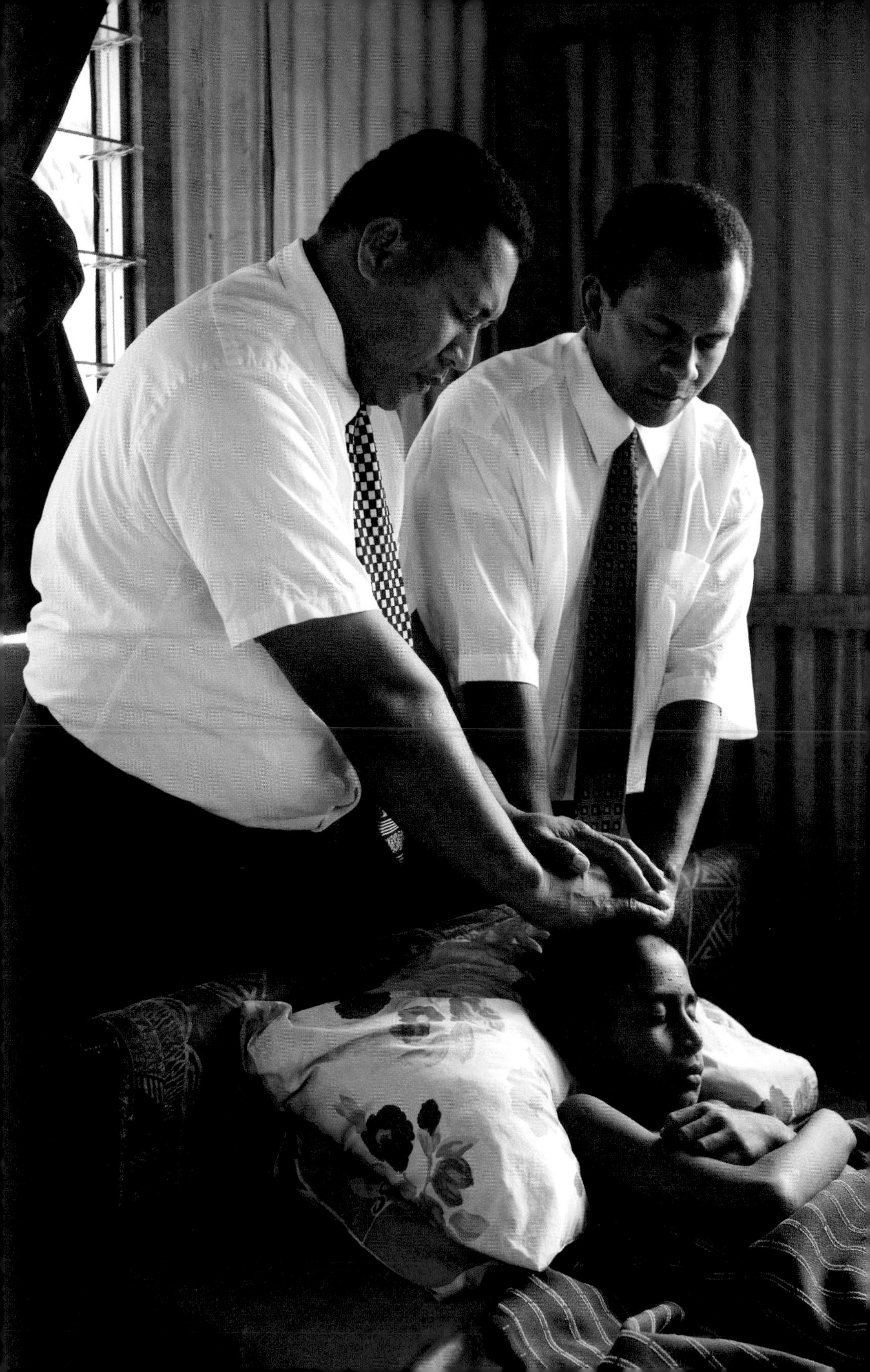

Men need the priesthood to preside in The Church of Jesus Christ of Latter-day Saints and to direct the work of the Church in all parts of the world. When Christ lived on the earth, He chose His Apostles and ordained them so that they could lead His Church. He gave them the power and authority of the priesthood to act in His name. (See Mark 3:13–15; John 15:16.)

Another reason the priesthood is needed on the earth is so we can understand the will of the Lord and carry out His purposes. God reveals His will to His authorized priesthood representative on the earth, the prophet. The prophet, who is President of the Church, serves as the spokesman for God to all members of the Church and all people on the earth.

- Why is it essential for a man to have proper authority when he performs an ordinance?

How Do Men Receive the Priesthood?

The Lord has prepared an orderly way for His priesthood to be given to His sons on the earth. A worthy male member of the Church receives the priesthood "by the laying on of hands by those who are in authority, to preach the Gospel and administer in the ordinances thereof" (Articles of Faith 1:5).

This is the same way men received the priesthood long ago, even in the days of Moses: "And no man taketh this honour unto himself, but he that is called of God, as was Aaron" (Hebrews 5:4). Aaron received the priesthood from Moses, his priesthood leader (see Exodus 28:1). Only those who hold the priesthood can ordain others, and they can do so only when authorized by those who hold the keys for that ordination (see chapter 14 in this book).

Men cannot buy and sell the power and authority of the priesthood. Nor can they take this authority upon themselves. In the New Testament we read of a man named Simon who lived when Christ's Apostles presided over the Church. Simon became converted and was baptized into the Church. Because he was a skillful magician, the people believed he had the power of God. But Simon did not have the priesthood, and he knew it.

Priesthood Organization

Chapter 14

The Priesthood Is on the Earth Today

The Church of Jesus Christ of Latter-day Saints is governed by the priesthood. The priesthood, which is always associated with God's work, "continueth in the church of God in all generations, and is without beginning of days or end of years" (D&C 84:17). It is upon the earth today. Men young and old are baptized into the Church, and when they are judged worthy they are ordained to the priesthood. They are given the authority to act for the Lord and do His work on the earth.

Two Divisions of Priesthood

- How did the Melchizedek and Aaronic Priesthoods get their names?

The priesthood is divided into two parts: the Melchizedek Priesthood and the Aaronic Priesthood (see D&C 107:1). "The first is called the Melchizedek Priesthood . . . because Melchizedek was such a great high priest.

"Before his day it was called *the Holy Priesthood, after the Order of the Son of God.*

"But out of respect or reverence to the name of the Supreme Being, to avoid the too frequent repetition of his name, they, the church, in ancient days, called that priesthood after Melchizedek, or the Melchizedek Priesthood" (D&C 107:2–4; italics in original).

The lesser priesthood is an appendage to the Melchizedek Priesthood. It is called the Aaronic Priesthood because it was conferred on Aaron and his sons throughout all their generations. Those who

---

For teachers: Use questions at the beginning of a section to start a discussion and send class members or family members to the text to find more information. Use questions at the end of a section to help class members or family members ponder and discuss the meaning of what they have read and apply it in their lives.

hold the Aaronic Priesthood have authority to administer the outward ordinances of the sacrament and baptism. (See D&C 20:46; 107:13–14, 20.)

Those holding the Melchizedek Priesthood have the power and authority to lead the Church and direct the preaching of the gospel in all parts of the world. They administer all the spiritual work of the Church (see D&C 84:19–22; 107:8). They direct the work done in the temples; they preside over wards, branches, stakes, and missions. The Lord's chosen prophet, the President of the Church, is the presiding high priest over the Melchizedek Priesthood (see D&C 107:65–67).

Keys of the Priesthood

- What is the difference between the priesthood and the keys of the priesthood? Which priesthood leaders receive keys?

There is a difference between being ordained to an office in the priesthood and receiving keys of the priesthood. President Joseph F. Smith taught:

"The Priesthood in general is the authority given to man to act for God. Every man ordained to any degree of the Priesthood has this authority delegated to him.

"But it is necessary that every act performed under this authority shall be done at the proper time and place, in the proper way, and after the proper order. The power of directing these labors constitutes the *keys* of the Priesthood. In their fulness, the keys are held by only one person at a time, the prophet and president of the Church. He may delegate any portion of this power to another, in which case that person holds the keys of that particular labor. Thus, the president of a temple, the president of a stake, the bishop of a ward, the president of a mission, the president of a quorum, each holds the keys of the labors performed in that particular body or locality. His Priesthood is not increased by this special appointment; . . . the president of an elders' quorum, for example, has no more Priesthood than any member of that quorum. But he holds the power of directing the official labors performed in the . . . quorum, or in other words, the *keys* of that division of that work" (*Teachings of Presidents of the Church: Joseph F. Smith* [1998], 141; italics in original).

• How do priesthood keys safeguard the Church?

The Offices and Duties of the Aaronic Priesthood

• In what ways do Aaronic Priesthood holders serve?

When the Aaronic Priesthood is conferred on a man or boy, he is ordained to an office in that priesthood. The offices in the Aaronic Priesthood are deacon, teacher, priest, and bishop. Each office carries duties and responsibilities. Each quorum is presided over by a quorum president, who teaches the members their duties and asks them to fill assignments.

Some men join the Church or become active after they have passed the usual age to receive the offices of this priesthood. They are usually ordained to an office in the Aaronic Priesthood and can soon be ordained to other offices as they remain worthy.

Deacon

A young man who has been baptized and confirmed a member of the Church and is worthy may be ordained to the office of deacon when he is 12 years old. The deacons are usually assigned to pass the sacrament to members of the Church, keep Church buildings and grounds in good order, act as messengers for priesthood leaders, and fulfill special assignments such as collecting fast offerings.

Teacher

A worthy young man may be ordained a teacher when he is 14 years old or older. Teachers have all the duties, rights, and powers of the office of deacon plus additional ones. Teachers in the Aaronic Priesthood are to help Church members live the commandments (see D&C 20:53–59). To help fulfill this responsibility, they are usually assigned to serve as home teachers. They visit the homes of Church members and encourage them to live the principles of the gospel. They have been commanded to teach the truths of the gospel from the scriptures (see D&C 42:12). Teachers also prepare the bread and water for the sacrament service.

Priest

A worthy young man may be ordained a priest when he is 16 years old or older. Priests have all the duties, rights, and powers of the offices of deacon and teacher plus some additional ones (see D&C 20:46–51). A priest may baptize. He may also administer the sacrament. He may ordain other priests, teachers, and deacons. A priest may take charge of meetings when there is no Melchizedek Priesthood holder present. He is to preach the gospel to those around him.

Bishop

A bishop is ordained and set apart to preside over the Aaronic Priesthood in a ward. He is the president of the priests quorum (see D&C 107:87–88). When he is acting in his Aaronic Priesthood office, a bishop deals primarily with temporal matters, such as administering finances and records and directing care for the poor and needy (see D&C 107:68).

A bishop is also ordained a high priest so he can preside over all members in the ward (see D&C 107:71–73; 68:15). A bishop is a judge in Israel (see D&C 107:74) and interviews members for temple recommends, priesthood ordinations, and other needs. It is his right to have the gift of discernment.

- How have you been blessed through the service of Aaronic Priesthood holders?

The Offices and Duties of the Melchizedek Priesthood

- In what ways do Melchizedek Priesthood holders serve?

The offices of the Melchizedek Priesthood are elder, high priest, patriarch, Seventy, and Apostle.

Elder

Elders are called to teach, expound, exhort, baptize, and watch over the Church (see D&C 20:42). All Melchizedek Priesthood holders are elders. They have the authority to bestow the gift of the Holy Ghost by the laying on of hands (see D&C 20:43). Elders should conduct meetings of the Church as they are led by the Holy Ghost (see D&C 20:45; 46:2). Elders may administer to the sick (see D&C 42:44) and bless little children (see D&C 20:70). Elders may preside over Church meetings when there is no high priest present (D&C 107:11).

High Priest

A high priest is given the authority to officiate in the Church and administer spiritual things (see D&C 107:10, 12). He may also officiate in all lesser offices (see D&C 68:19). Stake presidents, mission presidents, high councilors, bishops, and other leaders of the Church are ordained high priests.

Patriarch

Patriarchs are ordained by General Authorities, or by stake presidents when they are authorized by the Council of the Twelve, to give patriarchal blessings to members of the Church. These blessings give us some understanding of our callings on earth. They are the word of the Lord personally to us. Patriarchs are also ordained high priests. (See D&C 107:39–56.)

Seventy

Seventies are special witnesses of Jesus Christ to the world and assist in building up and regulating the Church under the direction of the First Presidency and Quorum of the Twelve Apostles (see D&C 107:25, 34, 38, 93–97).

Apostle

An Apostle is a special witness of the name of Jesus Christ in all the world (see D&C 107:23). The Apostles administer the affairs of the Church throughout the world. Those who are ordained to the office of Apostle in the Melchizedek Priesthood are usually set apart as members of the Quorum of the Twelve Apostles. Each one is given all the keys of the kingdom of God on earth, but only the senior Apostle, who is President of the Church, actively exercises all of the keys. The others act under his direction.

- How have you been blessed through the service of Melchizedek Priesthood holders?

The Quorums of the Aaronic Priesthood

The Lord has instructed that the holders of the priesthood be organized into quorums. A quorum is a body of brethren holding the same priesthood office.

There are three quorums of the Aaronic Priesthood:

1. The deacons quorum, which consists of up to 12 deacons (see D&C 107:85). The presidency of the deacons quorum is called by the bishop from among the quorum members.
2. The teachers quorum, which consists of up to 24 teachers (see D&C 107:86). The presidency of the teachers quorum is called by the bishop from among the quorum members.
3. The priests quorum, which consists of up to 48 priests (see D&C 107:87–88). It is presided over by the bishop of the ward to which the quorum belongs. The bishop is a high priest and thus also belongs to the high priests quorum.

Whenever the number specified for a quorum is exceeded, the quorum may be divided.

The Quorums of the Melchizedek Priesthood

At the general Church level, the members of the First Presidency form a quorum, as do the Twelve Apostles. The Seventies are also organized in quorums.

At the local Church level—in wards and branches and stakes and districts—Melchizedek Priesthood bearers are organized into the following quorums:

Elders Quorum

Each elders quorum "is instituted for standing ministers; nevertheless they may travel, yet they are ordained to be standing ministers" (D&C 124:137). They do most of their work near their homes. The quorum is to consist of up to 96 elders, presided over by a quorum presidency. When this number is exceeded, the quorum may be divided.

High Priests Quorum

Each quorum includes all high priests residing within the boundaries of a stake, including patriarchs and bishops. The stake president and his counselors are the presidency of this quorum. The high priests in each ward are organized into a group with a group leader.

Importance of Priesthood Quorums

- How can priesthood quorums help strengthen individuals and families?

When ordained to the priesthood, a man or boy automatically becomes a member of a priesthood quorum. From then on through life, it is expected that he will hold membership in a quorum of the priesthood according to his office (see Boyd K. Packer, "What Every Elder Should Know—and Every Sister as Well: A Primer on Principles of Priesthood Government," *Ensign,* Feb. 1993, 9).

If a priesthood quorum functions properly, the members of the quorum are encouraged, blessed, fellowshipped, and taught the gospel by their leaders. Even though a man may be released from Church callings, such as teacher, quorum president, bishop, high councilor, or stake president, his membership in his quorum does not change. Membership in a quorum of the priesthood should be regarded as a sacred privilege.

Auxiliaries to the Priesthood

- How can auxiliaries to the priesthood help strengthen individuals and families?

All organizations in the Church work under the direction of priesthood leaders and help them carry out the work of the Lord. For example, the presidencies in a ward's Relief Society, Young Women, Young Men, Primary, and Sunday School organizations serve under the direction of the bishopric. These organizations are called auxiliaries to the priesthood.

- What role do you have as an individual in helping priesthood quorums and auxiliaries be successful?

Additional Scriptures

- Alma 13:1–19 (manner in which men were ordained to the priesthood)
- Matthew 16:19; D&C 68:12 (Apostles given priesthood keys and power; what they seal on earth is sealed in heaven)
- D&C 20:38–67 (duties of elders, priests, teachers, deacons)
- D&C 84; 107 (revelations on the priesthood)
- 1 Corinthians 12:14–31 (all offices of the priesthood are important)

The Lord's Covenant People

Chapter 15

The Nature of Covenants

- What is a covenant? Why are Latter-day Saints called a covenant people?

From the beginning, the Lord has made covenants with His children on earth. When His people make covenants (or promises) with Him, they know what He expects of them and what blessings they may expect from Him. They can better carry out His work on earth. The people who covenant with the Lord and with whom the Lord makes covenants are known as the Lord's covenant people. Members of the Church are part of the Lord's covenant people.

Within the gospel, a covenant means a sacred agreement or mutual promise between God and a person or a group of people. In making a covenant, God promises a blessing for obedience to particular commandments. He sets the terms of His covenants, and He reveals these terms to His prophets. If we choose to obey the terms of the covenant, we receive promised blessings. If we choose not to obey, He withholds the blessings, and in some instances a penalty also is given.

For example, when we join the Church we make several covenants with God (see chapter 20 in this book). We covenant with the Savior at baptism to take upon ourselves His name. He promises that "as many as repent and are baptized in my name, which is Jesus Christ, and endure to the end, the same shall be saved" (D&C 18:22). We covenant with the Lord as we partake of the sacrament (see chapter 23 in this book). We promise to take His name upon ourselves, to remember Him, and to obey His commandments. We are promised

that the Holy Spirit will be with us. (See D&C 20:77–79.) When we receive temple ordinances, we make other sacred covenants and are promised exaltation for faithful obedience (see D&C 132; see also chapter 47 in this book).

God has also made special covenants with particular persons or groups. He made special covenants with Adam, Enoch, Noah, the children of Israel, and Lehi (see Moses 6:31–36, 52; Genesis 9:9–17; Exodus 19:5–6; 2 Nephi 1). He made a special covenant with Abraham and his descendants that blesses members of the Church and all nations of the earth today.

- Think about the covenants you have made with God and the blessings He has promised you for keeping these covenants.

God's Covenant with Abraham and His Descendants

- What is the Abrahamic covenant?

Abraham, an Old Testament prophet, was a very righteous man (see the picture in this chapter). He refused to worship his father's idols. He kept all of the Lord's commandments. Because of Abraham's righteousness, the Lord made a covenant with him and his descendants.

The Lord promised Abraham that he would have numberless descendants. He promised that all of them would be entitled to receive the gospel, the blessings of the priesthood, and all of the ordinances of exaltation. These descendants, through the power of the priesthood, would carry the gospel to all nations. Through them, all the families of the earth would be blessed (see Abraham 2:11). God further promised that if they were righteous He would establish His covenant with all generations of Abraham's children (see Genesis 17:4–8).

- How do the commandments and promises in the Abrahamic covenant apply to us? (Consider how this question applies in different settings, such as at home, in the workplace, in the community, or as missionaries.)

Members of the Church Are a Covenant People

- What blessings and responsibilities come to God's covenant people today?

The blood descendants of Abraham are not the only people whom God calls His covenant people. In speaking to Abraham, God said, "As many as receive this Gospel shall be called after thy name, and shall be accounted thy seed [lineage], and shall rise up and bless thee, as their father" (Abraham 2:10). Thus, two groups of people are included in the covenant made with Abraham: (1) Abraham's righteous blood descendants and (2) those adopted into his lineage by accepting and living the gospel of Jesus Christ (see 2 Nephi 30:2).

When we are baptized into the Church, we enter into the covenant the Lord made with Abraham, Isaac, and Jacob (see Galatians 3:26–29). If we are obedient, we inherit the blessings of that covenant. We have the right to receive help and guidance from the Holy Ghost. Worthy males have the right to hold the priesthood. Families can receive the blessings of the priesthood. We can gain eternal life in the celestial kingdom. There are no greater blessings than these.

Along with the blessings we receive as the Lord's covenant people, we have great responsibilities. The Lord promised Abraham that through his descendants the gospel would be taken to all the earth. We are fulfilling this responsibility through the full-time missionary program of the Church and the missionary work done by the members. This opportunity to preach the gospel to all the world belongs only to the Lord's Church and His covenant people.

As the Lord's covenant people, we should keep His commandments. The Lord said, "I, the Lord, am bound when ye do what I say; but when ye do not what I say, ye have no promise" (D&C 82:10). If we reject our covenant after accepting the gospel, the covenant becomes void and we will stand condemned before God (see D&C 132:4). He has said: "Refrain from sin, lest sore judgments fall upon your heads. For of him unto whom much is given much is

---

For teachers: You can help class members or family members think more deeply about a question by giving them time to ponder. After they have had enough time, ask for their responses.

required; and he who sins against the greater light shall receive the greater condemnation" (D&C 82:2–3).

The New and Everlasting Covenant

- What do we promise to do when we accept the gospel? What blessings does Heavenly Father give us as we keep these promises?

The fulness of the gospel is called the new and everlasting covenant. It includes the covenants made at baptism, during the sacrament, in the temple, and at any other time. The Lord calls it everlasting because it is ordained by an everlasting God and because the covenant will never be changed. He gave this same covenant to Adam, Enoch, Noah, Abraham, and other prophets. In this sense it is not new. But the Lord calls it new because each time the gospel is restored after being taken from the earth, it is new to the people who receive it (see Jeremiah 31:31–34; Ezekiel 37:26).

When we accept the new and everlasting covenant, we agree to repent, be baptized, receive the Holy Ghost, receive our endowments, receive the covenant of marriage in the temple, and follow and obey Christ to the end of our lives. As we keep our covenants, our Heavenly Father promises us that we will receive exaltation in the celestial kingdom (see D&C 132:20–24; see also chapter 47 in this book).

The greatness of that promise is hard for mortals to understand. The commandments He gives are for our benefit, and as we are faithful we may forever share the blessings and beauties of heaven and earth. We may live in His presence and partake of His love, compassion, power, greatness, knowledge, wisdom, glory, and dominions.

- What does being the Lord's covenant people have to do with how we dress, act, and keep the commandments of God?

Additional Scriptures and Other Sources

- 1 Peter 2:9–10 (peculiar people)
- D&C 54:4–6 (effects of covenants kept and broken)
- D&C 132:7 (covenants made by proper authority)

- D&C 133:57–60 (purpose of covenants)
- D&C 35:24 (promises for obedience to covenants)
- Hebrews 8:6 (Jesus Christ is the mediator of a better covenant)
- Bible Dictionary, "Covenant," 651

The Church of Jesus Christ in Former Times

Chapter 16

Some Features That Identify the Church of Jesus Christ

"We believe in the same organization that existed in the Primitive Church, namely, apostles, prophets, pastors, teachers, evangelists, and so forth" (Articles of Faith 1:6).

Jesus established His Church when He was on the earth. It was called the Church of Jesus Christ (see 3 Nephi 27:8), and the members were called Saints (see Ephesians 2:19–20).

Revelation

When Jesus established His Church, He personally instructed and directed its leaders. He, in turn, received His instructions from His Father in Heaven. (See Hebrews 1:1–2.) Thus the Church of Jesus Christ was directed by God and not by men. Jesus taught His followers that revelation was the "rock" upon which He would build His Church (see Matthew 16:16–18).

Before Jesus ascended into heaven after His Resurrection, He told His Apostles, "I am with you alway, even unto the end of the world" (Matthew 28:20). True to His word, He continued to guide them from heaven. He sent the Holy Ghost to be a comforter and a revelator to them (see Luke 12:12; John 14:26). He spoke to Saul in a vision (see Acts 9:3–6). He revealed to Peter that the gospel should be taught not only to the Jews but to the whole world (see Acts 10). He revealed many glorious truths to John, which

---

For teachers: Consider inviting each member of your family or class to study one of the six features that identify the Church—the italicized headings such as *Revelation* and *Authority from God.* (In large classes, some members will be assigned the same feature. In families and small classes, some members may be assigned more than one feature.) When they have had time to study, invite them to discuss what they have learned.

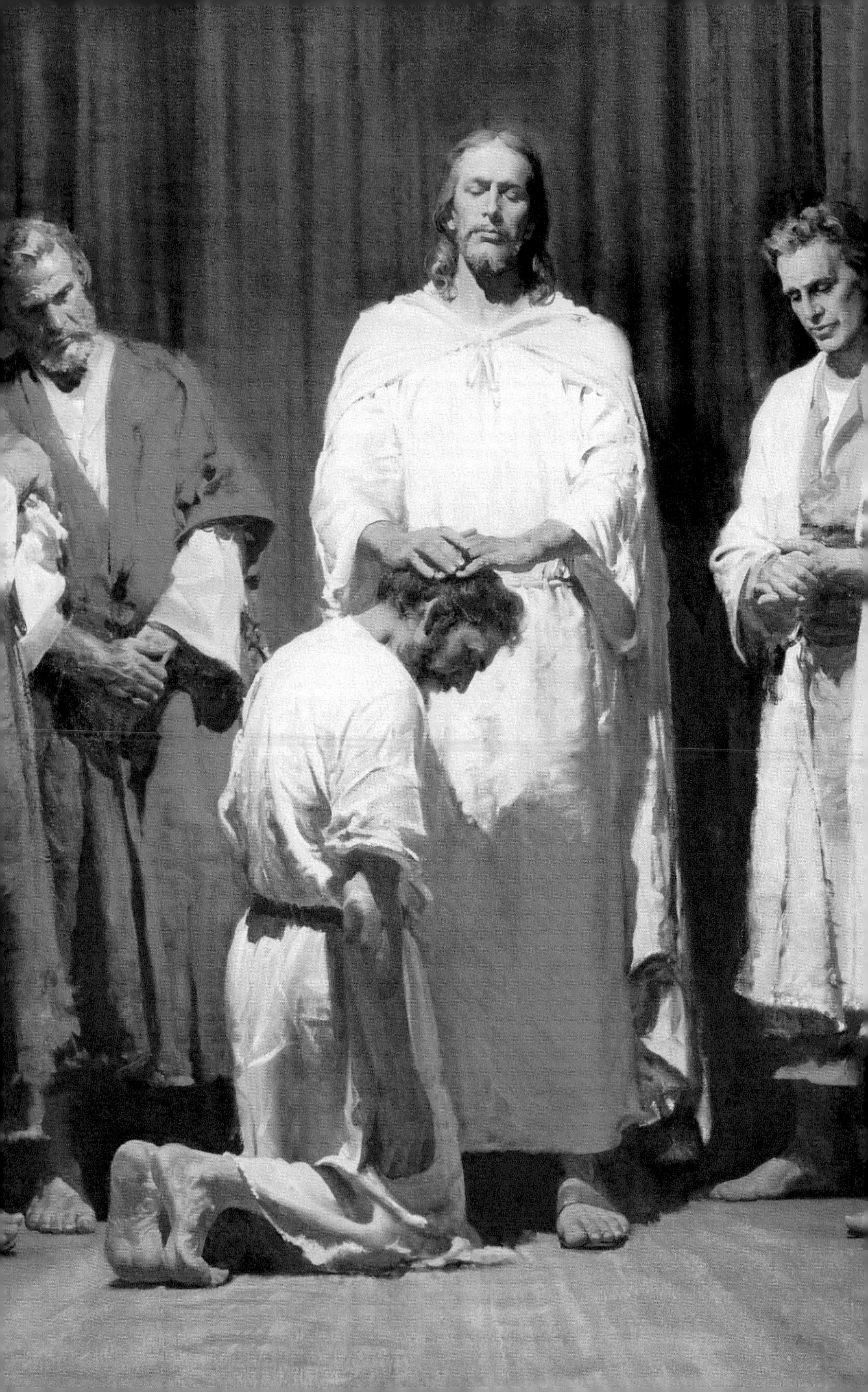

are written in the book of Revelation. The New Testament records many other ways in which Jesus revealed His will to guide His Church and enlighten His disciples.

Authority from God

The ordinances and principles of the gospel cannot be administered and taught without the priesthood. The Father gave this authority to Jesus Christ (see Hebrews 5:4–6), who in turn ordained His Apostles and gave them the power and authority of the priesthood (see Luke 9:1–2; Mark 3:14). He reminded them, "Ye have not chosen me, but I have chosen you, and ordained you" (John 15:16).

That there might be order in His Church, Jesus gave the greatest responsibility and authority to the Twelve Apostles. He appointed Peter chief Apostle and gave him the keys to seal blessings both on earth and in heaven (see Matthew 16:19). Jesus also ordained other officers with specific duties to perform. After He ascended into heaven, the pattern of appointment and ordination was continued. Others were ordained to the priesthood by those who had already received that authority. Jesus made it known through the Holy Ghost that He approved of those ordinations (see Acts 1:24).

The Church Organization

The Church of Jesus Christ was a carefully organized unit. It was compared to a building that was "built upon the foundation of the apostles and prophets, Jesus Christ himself being the chief corner stone" (Ephesians 2:20).

Jesus appointed other priesthood leaders to assist the Apostles in the work of the ministry. He sent officers called Seventies in pairs to preach the gospel (see Luke 10:1). Other officers in the Church were evangelists (patriarchs), pastors (presiding leaders), high priests, elders, bishops, priests, teachers, and deacons (see chapter 14 in this book). These officers were all necessary to do missionary work, perform ordinances, and instruct and inspire Church members. These officers helped the members come to a "unity of the faith, and of the knowledge of the Son of God" (Ephesians 4:13).

The Bible does not tell us everything about the priesthood or the organization and government of the Church. However, enough of the Bible has been preserved to show the beauty and perfection of the Church organization. The Apostles were commanded to go into all the world and preach (see Matthew 28:19–20). They could not stay in any one city to supervise new converts. Therefore, local priesthood leaders were called and ordained, and the Apostles presided over them. The Apostles and other Church leaders visited and wrote letters to the various branches. Thus, our New Testament contains letters written by Paul, Peter, James, John, and Jude, giving counsel and instruction to the local priesthood leaders.

The New Testament shows that this Church organization was intended to continue. For example, the death of Judas left only eleven Apostles. Soon after Jesus had ascended into heaven, the eleven Apostles met together to choose someone to take the place of Judas. Through revelation from the Holy Ghost, they chose Matthias. (See Acts 1:23–26.) Jesus had set a pattern for twelve Apostles to govern the Church. It seemed clear that the organization was to continue as He had established it.

First Principles and Ordinances

The Apostles taught two basic principles: faith in the Lord Jesus Christ and repentance. After new converts had faith in Jesus Christ as the Son of God and their Redeemer and had repented of their sins, they received two ordinances: baptism by immersion and the laying on of hands for the gift of the Holy Ghost (see Acts 19:1–6). These were the first principles and ordinances of the gospel. Jesus had taught, "Except a man be born of water and of the Spirit, he cannot enter into the kingdom of God" (John 3:5).

Ordinances Performed for the Dead

Jesus has provided for everyone to hear the gospel, whether on earth or after death. Between His death and Resurrection, Jesus went among the spirits of those who had died. He organized missionary work among those who were dead. He appointed righteous messengers and gave them power to teach the gospel to all the spirits of people who had died. This gave them an opportunity to accept the gospel. (See 1 Peter 3:18–20; 4:6; D&C 138.) Living members of His Church then performed ordinances in behalf of the dead (see 1 Corinthians 15:29). Ordinances such as baptism and confirmation must be done on earth.

Spiritual Gifts

All faithful members of the Church were entitled to receive gifts of the Spirit. These were given to them according to their individual needs, capacities, and assignments. Some of these gifts were faith, including the power to heal and to be healed; prophecy; and visions. (The gifts of the Spirit are discussed in more detail in chapter 22.) Spiritual gifts always exist in the true Church of Jesus Christ (see 1 Corinthians 12:4–11; Moroni 10:8–18; D&C 46:8–29). Jesus told His disciples that these signs or spiritual gifts always follow them that believe (see Mark 16:17–18). Many of His disciples performed miracles, prophesied, or beheld visions through the power of the Holy Ghost.

- Why does the Church of Jesus Christ need these six features?

The Church of Jesus Christ in the Americas

After Jesus was resurrected, He visited the people in the Americas and organized His Church among them, teaching the people for three days and then returning often for some time thereafter (see 3 Nephi 11–28). Then He left them and ascended into heaven. For over 200 years they lived righteously and were among the happiest people whom God had created (see 4 Nephi 1:16).

Apostasy from the True Church

- What does the term *apostasy* mean?

Throughout history, evil people have tried to destroy the work of God. This happened while the Apostles were still alive and supervising the young, growing Church. Some members taught ideas from their old pagan or Jewish beliefs instead of the simple truths taught by Jesus. Some rebelled openly. In addition, there was persecution from outside the Church. Church members were tortured and killed for their beliefs. One by one, the Apostles were killed or otherwise taken from the earth. Because of wickedness and apostasy, the apostolic authority and priesthood keys were also taken from the earth. The organization that Jesus Christ had established no longer existed, and confusion resulted. More and more error crept into Church doctrine, and soon the dissolution of the Church was complete. The period of time when the true Church no longer existed on earth is called the Great Apostasy.

Soon pagan beliefs dominated the thinking of those called Christians. The Roman emperor adopted this false Christianity as the state religion. This church was very different from the church Jesus organized. It taught that God was a being without form or substance.

These people lost the understanding of God's love for us. They did not know that we are His children. They did not understand the purpose of life. Many of the ordinances were changed because the priesthood and revelation were no longer on the earth.

The emperor chose his own leaders and sometimes called them by the same titles used by priesthood leaders in the true Church of Christ. There were no Apostles or other priesthood leaders with power from God, and there were no spiritual gifts. The prophet Isaiah had foreseen this condition, prophesying, "The earth also is defiled under the inhabitants thereof; because they have transgressed the laws, changed the ordinance, broken the everlasting covenant" (Isaiah 24:5). It was the Church of Jesus Christ no longer; it was a church of men. Even the name had been changed. In the Americas, apostasy also occurred (see 4 Nephi).

A Restoration Foretold

- What prophecies in the Old and New Testaments foretold the Restoration?

God had foreseen the Apostasy and prepared for the gospel to be restored. The Apostle Peter spoke of this to the Jews: "He shall send Jesus Christ, which before was preached unto you: whom the heaven must receive until the times of restitution of all things, which God hath spoken by the mouth of all his holy prophets since the world began" (Acts 3:20–21).

John the Revelator had also foreseen the time when the gospel would be restored. He said, "I saw another angel fly in the midst of heaven, having the everlasting gospel to preach unto them that dwell on the earth, and to every nation, and kindred, and tongue, and people" (Revelation 14:6).

- Why was the Restoration necessary?
- Consider the blessings that have come to you because the Church of Jesus Christ has been restored to the earth.

Additional Scriptures

- Ephesians 2:19 (members called Saints)
- 1 Corinthians 12:12–31 (Church likened to a body)
- Luke 10:1; Acts 14:23; Titus 1:7; 1 Timothy 2:7 (officers of the Church identified)
- John 8:26–29 (the Father directs Jesus)
- Luke 9:1; James 1:17; 5:14–15 (spiritual gifts)
- Mosiah 27:13 (apostasy comes as a result of transgression)
- 2 Peter 2:1; Matthew 24:9–12; John 16:1–3; Amos 8:11; 2 Thessalonians 2:3–4 (Apostasy predicted)
- Daniel 2:44–45; Matthew 24:14; Acts 3:19–21; Micah 4:1; Isaiah 2:2–4 (Restoration predicted)

The Church of Jesus Christ Today

Chapter 17

The Church of Jesus Christ Was Taken from the Earth

- Why was the Church of Jesus Christ removed from the earth shortly after the Savior's death and Resurrection?

When Jesus lived on the earth, He established His Church, the only true Church. He organized His Church so the truths of the gospel could be taught to all people and the ordinances of the gospel could be administered correctly with authority. Through this organization, Christ could bring the blessings of salvation to mankind.

After the Savior ascended into heaven, men changed the ordinances and doctrines that He and His Apostles had established. Because of apostasy, there was no direct revelation from God. The true Church was no longer on the earth. Men organized different churches that claimed to be true but taught conflicting doctrines. There was much confusion and contention over religion. The Lord had foreseen these conditions of apostasy, saying there would be "a famine in the land, not a famine of bread, nor a thirst for water, but of hearing the words of the Lord. . . . They shall . . . seek the word of the Lord, and shall not find it" (Amos 8:11–12).

- How does the famine spoken of in Amos 8:11–12 affect people?

The Lord Promised to Restore His True Church

- What were some of the conditions in the world that prepared the way for the Restoration of the gospel?

The Savior promised to restore His Church in the latter days. He said, "I will proceed to do a marvellous work among this people, even a marvellous work and a wonder" (Isaiah 29:14).

For many years people lived in spiritual darkness. About 1,700 years after Christ, people were becoming more and more interested in knowing the truth about God and religion. Some of them could see that the gospel Jesus taught was no longer on the earth. Some recognized that there was no revelation and no true authority and that the Church that Christ organized did not exist on the earth. The time had arrived for the Church of Jesus Christ to be restored to the earth.

- In what ways is the Restoration of the fulness of the gospel a "marvellous work"?

New Revelation from God

- When Joseph Smith received his First Vision, what did he learn about God?

In the spring of 1820, one of the most important events in the history of the world occurred. The time had come for the marvelous work and wonder of which the Lord had spoken. As a young boy, Joseph Smith wanted to know which of all the churches was the true Church of Jesus Christ. He went into the woods near his home and prayed humbly and intently to his Heavenly Father, asking which church he should join. On that morning a miraculous thing happened. Heavenly Father and Jesus Christ appeared to Joseph Smith. The Savior told him not to join any church because the true Church was not on the earth. He also said that the creeds of present churches were "an abomination in his sight" (Joseph Smith—History 1:19; see also verses 7–18, 20). Beginning with this event, there was again direct revelation from the heavens. The Lord had chosen a new prophet. Since that time the heavens have not been closed. Revelation continues to this day through each of His chosen prophets. Joseph was to be the one to help restore the true gospel of Jesus Christ.

- Why was the First Vision one of the most important events in the history of the world?

Authority from God Was Restored

- Why was the restoration of the Aaronic and Melchizedek Priesthoods necessary?

In restoring the gospel, God again gave the priesthood to men. John the Baptist came in 1829 to confer the Aaronic Priesthood on Joseph Smith and Oliver Cowdery (see D&C 13; 27:8). Then Peter, James, and John, the presidency of the Church in ancient times, came and gave Joseph and Oliver the Melchizedek Priesthood and the keys of the kingdom of God (see D&C 27:12–13). Later, additional keys of the priesthood were restored by heavenly messengers such as Moses, Elias, and Elijah (see D&C 110:11–16). Through the Restoration, the priesthood was returned to the earth. Those who hold this priesthood today have the authority to perform ordinances such as baptism. They also have the authority to direct the Lord's kingdom on earth.

Christ's Church Was Organized Again

- What events led to the organization of the Church on the earth again?

On April 6, 1830, the Savior again directed the organizing of His Church on the earth (see D&C 20:1). His Church is called The Church of Jesus Christ of Latter-day Saints (see D&C 115:4). Christ is the head of His Church today, just as He was in ancient times. The Lord has said that it is "the only true and living church upon the face of the whole earth, with which I, the Lord, am well pleased" (D&C 1:30).

Joseph Smith was sustained as prophet and "first elder" of the Church (see D&C 20:2–4). Later the First Presidency was organized, and he was sustained as President. When the Church was first organized, only the framework was set up. The organization would develop as the Church continued to grow.

The Church was organized with the same offices as were in the ancient Church. That organization included apostles, prophets,

---

For teachers: Bearing testimony invites the Spirit. As part of this lesson, bear your testimony of the Restoration and give others the opportunity to do the same.

seventies, evangelists (patriarchs), pastors (presiding officers), high priests, elders, bishops, priests, teachers, and deacons. These same offices are in His Church today (see Articles of Faith 1:6).

A prophet, acting under the direction of the Lord, leads the Church. This prophet is also the President of the Church. He holds all the authority necessary to direct the Lord's work on earth (see D&C 107:65, 91). Two counselors assist the President. Twelve Apostles, who are special witnesses of the name of Jesus Christ, teach the gospel and regulate the affairs of the Church in all parts of the world. Other general officers of the Church with special assignments, including the Presiding Bishopric and the Quorums of the Seventy, serve under the direction of the First Presidency and the Twelve.

The offices of the priesthood include apostles, seventies, patriarchs, high priests, bishops, elders, priests, teachers, and deacons. These are the same offices that existed in the original Church.

The Church has grown much larger than it was in the days of Jesus. As it has grown, the Lord has revealed additional units of organization within the Church. When the Church is fully organized in an area, it has local divisions called stakes. A stake president and his two counselors preside over each stake. The stake has 12 high councilors who help do the Lord's work in the stake. Melchizedek Priesthood quorums are organized in the stake under the direction of the stake president (see chapter 14 in this book). Each stake is divided into smaller areas called wards. A bishop and his two counselors preside over each ward.

In areas of the world where the Church is developing, there are districts, which are like stakes. Districts are divided into smaller units called branches, which are like wards.

Important Truths Were Restored

- What important truths have been brought back with the Restoration of the Church?

The Church today teaches the same principles and performs the same ordinances as were performed in the days of Jesus. The first principles and ordinances of the gospel are faith in the Lord

As we carefully study the scriptures, we learn that faith is a strong belief of truth within our souls that motivates us to do good. This causes us to ask: In whom should we have faith?

- Think about your everyday activities. What are things you act upon each day that you cannot see the end results of? How does faith move you to action?

Why Should We Have Faith in Jesus Christ?

We must center our faith in the Lord Jesus Christ.

To have faith in Jesus Christ means to have such trust in Him that we obey whatever He commands. As we place our faith in Jesus Christ, becoming His obedient disciples, Heavenly Father will forgive our sins and prepare us to return to Him.

The Apostle Peter preached that "there is none other name under heaven given among men, whereby we must be saved" (Acts 4:12; see also Mosiah 3:17). Jacob taught that men must have "perfect faith in the Holy One of Israel [Jesus Christ], or they cannot be saved in the kingdom of God" (2 Nephi 9:23). Through faith in the Savior and through repentance, we make His Atonement fully effective in our lives. Through faith we can also receive strength to overcome temptations (see Alma 37:33).

We cannot have faith in Jesus Christ without also having faith in our Heavenly Father. If we have faith in Them, we will also have faith that the Holy Ghost, whom They send, will teach us all truth and will comfort us.

- How can faith in Jesus Christ influence us in our Church callings? in our family relationships? in our jobs? How does faith in Jesus Christ influence our hope for eternal life?

How Can We Increase Our Faith in Jesus Christ?

Knowing of the many blessings that come through exercising faith in Jesus Christ, we should seek to increase our faith in Him. The Savior said, "If ye have faith as a grain of mustard seed, . . . nothing shall be impossible unto you" (Matthew 17:20). A mustard seed is very small, but it grows into a large tree.

earth; for these are the effects of faith. . . . And he who possesses it will, through it, obtain all necessary knowledge and wisdom, until he shall know God, and the Lord Jesus Christ, whom he has sent—whom to know is eternal life" (*Lectures on Faith* [1985], 83).

- What are some stories from the scriptures in which people have become stronger because they had faith in Jesus Christ? How have you seen this happen in your own life?

Additional Scriptures

- Hebrews 11; Alma 32 (nature of faith explained)
- Exodus 14:19–22 (parting the waters of the Red Sea)
- Genesis 6–8 (Noah and the flood)
- Matthew 8:5–33 (sick healed, tempest calmed, miracles of faith)
- Mark 5:25–34 (healed by faith)
- Romans 10:17 (faith comes by hearing the word of God)

Repentance

Chapter 19

We All Need to Repent

- What is sin? What effects do our sins have on us?

Faith in Jesus Christ naturally leads to repentance. There has been the need for repentance in the world from the time of Adam to the present day. The Lord instructed Adam, "Wherefore teach it unto your children, that all men, everywhere, must repent, or they can in nowise inherit the kingdom of God, for no unclean thing can dwell there, or dwell in his presence" (Moses 6:57).

We come to earth for the purpose of growing and progressing. This is a lifelong process. During this time we all sin (see Romans 3:23). We all have need to repent. Sometimes we sin because of ignorance, sometimes because of our weaknesses, and sometimes because of willful disobedience. In the Bible we read that "there is not a just man upon earth, that doeth good, and sinneth not" (Ecclesiastes 7:20) and that "if we say that we have no sin, we deceive ourselves, and the truth is not in us" (1 John 1:8).

What is sin? James said, "To him that knoweth to do good, and doeth it not, to him it is sin" (James 4:17). John described sin as "all unrighteousness" (1 John 5:17) and "the transgression of the law" (1 John 3:4).

That is why the Lord said, "All men, everywhere, must repent" (Moses 6:57). Except for Jesus Christ, who lived a perfect life, everyone who has lived upon the earth has sinned. Our Heavenly Father in His great love has provided us this opportunity to repent of our sins.

Becoming Free from Our Sins through Repentance

• What is repentance?

Repentance is the way provided for us to become free from our sins and receive forgiveness for them. Sins slow our spiritual progression and can even stop it. Repentance makes it possible for us to grow and develop spiritually again.

The privilege of repenting is made possible through the Atonement of Jesus Christ. In a way we do not fully understand, Jesus paid for our sins. President Joseph Fielding Smith said of this:

"I have suffered pain, you have suffered pain, and sometimes it has been quite severe; but I cannot comprehend pain . . . that would cause the blood, like sweat, to come out upon the body. It was something terrible, something terrific. . . .

". . . There was *no man ever born into this world that could have stood under the weight of the load that was upon the Son of God, when he was carrying my sins and yours* and making it possible that we might escape from our sins" (*Doctrines of Salvation,* sel. Bruce R. McConkie, 3 vols. [1954–56], 1:130–31; italics in original).

Repentance sometimes requires great courage, much strength, many tears, unceasing prayers, and untiring efforts to live the commandments of the Lord.

Principles of Repentance

• What are the principles of repentance?

President Spencer W. Kimball declared: "There is *no royal road to repentance,* no privileged path to forgiveness. Every man must follow the same course whether he be rich or poor, educated or untrained, tall or short, prince or pauper, king or commoner" (*Teachings of Presidents of the Church: Spencer W. Kimball* [2006], 38; italics in original).

For teachers: Writing a list can generate interest and help learners focus their attention. As you discuss the principles of repentance with class members or family members, you may want to ask someone to write the principles on the board or on a large piece of paper.

We Must Recognize Our Sins

To repent, we must admit to ourselves that we have sinned. If we do not admit this, we cannot repent.

Alma counseled his son Corianton, who had been unfaithful in his missionary calling and had committed serious sins: "Let your sins trouble you, with that trouble which shall bring you down unto repentance. . . . Do not endeavor to excuse yourself in the least point" (Alma 42:29–30). The scriptures advise us further not to justify our sinful practices (see Luke 16:15–16).

We cannot hide any act of our lives from ourselves or from the Lord.

We Must Feel Sorrow for Our Sins

In addition to recognizing our sins, we must feel sincere sorrow for what we have done. We must feel that our sins are terrible. We must want to unload and abandon them. The scriptures tell us, "All those who humble themselves before God, and desire to be baptized, and come forth with broken hearts and contrite spirits, and . . . have truly repented of all their sins . . . shall be received by baptism into his church" (D&C 20:37).

- Study 2 Corinthians 7:9–10 and Mormon 2:10–14. In what ways do you think "godly sorrow" is different from expressions of regret?

We Must Forsake Our Sins

Our sincere sorrow should lead us to forsake (stop) our sins. If we have stolen something, we will steal no more. If we have lied, we will lie no more. If we have committed adultery, we will stop. The Lord revealed to the Prophet Joseph Smith, "By this ye may know if a man repenteth of his sins—behold, he will confess them and forsake them" (D&C 58:43).

We Must Confess Our Sins

Confessing our sins is very important. The Lord has commanded us to confess our sins. Confession relieves a heavy burden from the sinner. The Lord has promised, "I, the Lord, forgive sins, and am merciful unto those who confess their sins with humble hearts" (D&C 61:2).

We must confess all our sins to the Lord. In addition, we must confess serious sins—such as adultery, fornication, homosexual relations, spouse or child abuse, and the sale or use of illegal drugs—which might affect our standing in the Church, to the proper priesthood authority. If we have sinned against another person, we should confess to the person we have injured. Some less serious sins involve no one but ourselves and the Lord. These may be confessed privately to the Lord.

We Must Make Restitution

Part of repentance is to make restitution. This means that as much as possible we must make right any wrong that we have done. For example, a thief should give back what he has stolen. A liar should make the truth known. A gossip who has slandered the character of a person should work to restore the good name of the person he has harmed. As we do these things, God will not mention our sins to us when we are judged (see Ezekiel 33:15–16).

We Must Forgive Others

A vital part of repentance is to forgive those who have sinned against us. The Lord will not forgive us unless our hearts are fully cleansed of all hate, bitterness, and bad feelings against other people (see 3 Nephi 13:14–15). "Wherefore, I say unto you, that ye ought to forgive one another; for he that forgiveth not his brother his trespasses standeth condemned before the Lord; for there remaineth in him the greater sin" (D&C 64:9).

We Must Keep the Commandments of God

To make our repentance complete we must keep the commandments of the Lord (see D&C 1:32). We are not fully repentant if we do not pay tithes or keep the Sabbath day holy or obey the Word of Wisdom. We are not repentant if we do not sustain the authorities of the Church and do not love the Lord and our fellowmen. If we do not pray and are unkind to others, we are surely not repentant. When we repent, our life changes.

President Kimball said: "First, one repents. Having gained that ground he then must live the commandments of the Lord to retain his vantage point. This is necessary to secure complete forgiveness" (*Teachings of Presidents of the Church: Spencer W. Kimball,* 43).

- How do the teachings in this section differ from the false idea that repentance is the performance of a list of simple steps or routine actions?

How Repentance Helps Us

- In what ways does repentance help us?

As we repent, the Atonement of Jesus Christ becomes fully effective in our lives, and the Lord forgives our sins. We become free from the bondage of our sins, and we find joy.

Alma recounted his experience of repenting from his sinful past:

"My soul was harrowed up [troubled] to the greatest degree and racked with all my sins.

"Yea, I did remember all my sins and iniquities, for which I was tormented with the pains of hell; yea, I saw that I had rebelled against my God, and that I had not kept his holy commandments.

". . . So great had been my iniquities, that the very thought of coming into the presence of my God did rack my soul with inexpressible horror.

". . . It came to pass that as I was . . . harrowed up by the memory of my many sins, behold, I remembered also to have heard my father prophesy . . . concerning the coming of one Jesus Christ, a Son of God, to atone for the sins of the world.

"Now, as my mind caught hold upon this thought, I cried within my heart: O Jesus, thou Son of God, have mercy on me. . . .

"And now, behold, when I thought this, I could remember my pains no more. . . .

"And oh, what joy, and what marvelous light I did behold; yea, my soul was filled with joy as exceeding as was my pain!

". . . There can be nothing so exquisite and sweet as was my joy" (Alma 36:12–14, 17–21).

- How did repentance and forgiveness bring Alma joy?

The Dangers of Procrastinating Our Repentance

- What are some possible consequences of procrastinating our repentance?

The prophets have declared that "this life is the time for men to prepare to meet God" (Alma 34:32). We should repent now, every day. When we get up in the morning, we should examine ourselves to see whether the Spirit of God is with us. At night before we go to sleep, we should review our acts and words of the day and ask the Lord to help us recognize the things for which we need to repent. By repenting every day and having the Lord forgive our sins, we will experience the daily process of becoming perfect. As with Alma, our happiness and joy can be sweet and exquisite.

Additional Scriptures

- Matthew 9:10–13; Luke 13:3; Ezekiel 18:30 (repent or perish)
- Alma 7:21 (no unclean thing can dwell in God's presence)
- 2 Corinthians 7:9–10 (godly sorrow)
- Mosiah 4:10–12 (steps to repentance)
- Isaiah 1:18; Mosiah 26:28–32 (repentance brings forgiveness)
- D&C 58:42 (sins remembered no more)
- 2 Nephi 9:23 (repentance necessary to salvation)
- 2 Nephi 2:21 (repent while in the flesh)
- D&C 19:15–20 (the Lord has commanded us to repent so we will not have to suffer as He did)

Baptism

Chapter 20

The Commandment to Be Baptized

• Why must we be baptized?

Today, as in the days of Jesus, there are certain principles and ordinances of the gospel that we must learn and obey. A gospel principle is a true belief or teaching. An ordinance is a rite or a ceremony. The first two principles of the gospel are faith in the Lord Jesus Christ and repentance. Baptism is the first ordinance of the gospel. One of the instructions the Lord gave His Apostles was, "Go ye therefore, and teach all nations, baptizing them in the name of the Father, and of the Son, and of the Holy Ghost: teaching them to observe all things whatsoever I have commanded you" (Matthew 28:19–20).

We Must Be Baptized for the Remission of Our Sins

When we place our faith in Jesus Christ, repent, and are baptized, our sins are forgiven through the Atonement of Jesus Christ.

From the scriptures we learn that John the Baptist "did baptize in the wilderness, and preach the baptism of repentance for the remission of sins" (Mark 1:4). The Apostle Peter taught, "Repent, and be baptized every one of you in the name of Jesus Christ for the remission of sins" (Acts 2:38). Following Paul's conversion, Ananias said to him, "Arise, and be baptized, and wash away thy sins" (Acts 22:16).

We Must Be Baptized to Become Members of the Church of Jesus Christ

"All those who humble themselves before God, and desire to be baptized . . . that . . . have truly repented of all their sins . . . shall be received by baptism into his church" (D&C 20:37).

For teachers: Use questions at the beginning of a section to start a discussion and send class members or family members to the text to find more information. Use questions at the end of a section to help class members or family members ponder and discuss the meaning of what they have read and apply it in their lives.

We Must Be Baptized before We Can Receive the Gift of the Holy Ghost

The Lord said, "If thou wilt turn unto me, and . . . repent of all thy transgressions [sins], and be baptized, even in water, in the name of mine Only Begotten Son, . . . ye shall receive the gift of the Holy Ghost" (Moses 6:52).

We Must Be Baptized to Show Obedience

Jesus Christ was without sin, yet He was baptized. He said His baptism was necessary "to fulfil all righteousness" (Matthew 3:15). The prophet Nephi explained that the Lord told him, "Follow me, and do the things which ye have seen me do . . . with full purpose of heart, acting no hypocrisy and no deception before God, but with real intent, repenting of your sins, witnessing unto the Father that ye are willing to take upon you the name of Christ, by baptism" (2 Nephi 31:12–13).

We Must Be Baptized to Enter the Celestial Kingdom

Jesus said, "Whoso believeth in me, and is baptized . . . shall inherit the kingdom of God. And whoso believeth not in me, and is not baptized, shall be damned" (3 Nephi 11:33–34). Baptism is the gateway through which we enter the path to the celestial kingdom (see 2 Nephi 31:17–18).

The Correct Mode of Baptism

• How should we be baptized?

There is only one correct mode of baptism. Jesus revealed to the Prophet Joseph Smith that a person having the proper priesthood authority to baptize "shall go down into the water with the person who has presented himself or herself for baptism. . . . Then shall he immerse him or her in the water, and come forth again out of the water" (D&C 20:73–74). Immersion is necessary. The Apostle Paul taught that being immersed in water and coming out again is symbolic of death, burial, and resurrection. After baptism we start a new life. Paul said:

"Know ye not, that so many of us as were baptized into Jesus Christ were baptized into his death?

"Therefore we are buried with him by baptism into death: that like as Christ was raised up from the dead by the glory of the Father, even so we also should walk in newness of life.

"For if we have been planted together in the likeness of his death, we shall be also in the likeness of his resurrection" (Romans 6:3–5).

Baptism by immersion by a person having the proper authority is the only acceptable way of being baptized.

- Why is authority to perform a baptism important?
- In what ways is baptism by immersion like the burial and Resurrection of the Savior?

Baptism at the Age of Accountability

- Who should be baptized?

Every person who has reached eight years of age and is accountable (responsible) for his or her actions should be baptized. Some churches teach that little children should be baptized. This is not in keeping with the teachings of the Savior. When Jesus spoke of little children, He said, "Of such is the kingdom of heaven" (Matthew 19:14).

The prophet Mormon said that it is mockery before God to baptize little children, because they are not capable of sinning. Likewise, baptism is not required of people who are mentally incapable of knowing right and wrong (see Moroni 8:9–22).

All other people are to be baptized. We must receive the ordinance of baptism and remain true to the covenants we make at that time.

- What might you say to a friend who believes that infants need to be baptized?

We Make Covenants When We Are Baptized

Many scriptures teach about baptism. In one of these scriptures, the prophet Alma taught that faith and repentance are steps that prepare us for baptism. He taught that when we are baptized we make a covenant with the Lord. We promise to do certain things, and God promises to bless us in return.

Alma explained that we must want to be called the people of God. We must be willing to help and comfort each other. We must stand as witnesses of God at all times and in all things and in all places. As we do these things and are baptized, God will forgive our sins. Alma told the people who believed his teachings about the gospel:

"Behold, here are the waters of Mormon. . . . And now, as ye are desirous to come into the fold of God, and to be called his people, . . . what have you against being baptized in the name of the Lord, as a witness before him that ye have entered into a covenant with him, that ye will serve him and keep his commandments, that he may pour out his Spirit more abundantly upon you?" (Mosiah 18:8, 10). The people clapped their hands for joy and said it was their desire to be baptized. Alma baptized them in the Waters of Mormon. (See Mosiah 18:7–17.)

Alma taught that when we are baptized we make covenants with the Lord to:

1. Come into the fold of God.
2. Bear one another's burdens.
3. Stand as witnesses of God at all times and in all places.
4. Serve God and keep His commandments.

When we are baptized and keep the covenants of baptism, the Lord promises to:

1. Forgive our sins (see Acts 2:38; D&C 49:13).
2. Pour out His Spirit more abundantly upon us (see Mosiah 18:10).
3. Give us daily guidance and the help of the Holy Ghost (see Acts 2:38; D&C 20:77).
4. Let us come forth in the First Resurrection (see Mosiah 18:9).
5. Give us eternal life (see Mosiah 18:9).

- What do you think it means to bear one another's burdens? to stand as a witness of God at all times and in all places?

Baptism Gives Us a New Beginning

With baptism we begin a new way of life. That is why we call it a rebirth. Jesus said that unless we are born of the water and of the Spirit, we cannot enter the kingdom of God (see John 3:3–5). This principle was explained clearly to Adam:

"Inasmuch as ye were born into the world by water, and blood, and the spirit, which I have made, and so became of dust a living soul, even so ye must be born again into the kingdom of heaven, of water, and of the Spirit, and be cleansed by blood, even the blood of mine Only Begotten" (Moses 6:59).

The Apostle Paul said that after our baptism we should begin a new life: "We are buried with him by baptism; . . . even so we also should walk in newness of life" (Romans 6:4). One of the great blessings of baptism is that it provides us with a new start on our way toward our eternal goal.

- How was your baptism a new beginning?

Additional Scriptures

- 2 Nephi 31:4–7 (purpose and necessity of baptism)
- 3 Nephi 11:21–27; D&C 20:72–74 (how to perform a baptism)
- Acts 2:38–39 (be baptized for the remission of sins)
- Moroni 8:8–12; D&C 20:71–72 (baptism is not required of little children; baptism is required of all who repent)
- Alma 7:14–16 (baptism is cleansing, entering into a covenant of eternal life)

The Gift of the Holy Ghost

Chapter 21

The Holy Ghost

In chapter 7 we learned that the Holy Ghost is a member of the Godhead. He is "a personage of Spirit" (D&C 130:22). He does not have a body of flesh and bones. His influence can be everywhere at once. His mission is to bear witness of the Father and the Son and of all truth. Furthermore, the Holy Ghost purifies, or sanctifies, us to prepare us to dwell in the presence of God. The Holy Ghost purifies our hearts so we no longer have the desire to do evil.

There is a difference between the Holy Ghost and the *gift* of the Holy Ghost. In this chapter we will learn what the gift of the Holy Ghost is and how we can receive this great gift from God.

The Gift of the Holy Ghost

- What is the difference between the Holy Ghost and the gift of the Holy Ghost?

The gift of the Holy Ghost is the privilege—given to people who have placed their faith in Jesus Christ, been baptized, and been confirmed as members of the Church—to receive continual guidance and inspiration from the Holy Ghost.

Joseph Smith said we believe in the gift of the Holy Ghost being enjoyed now as much as it was enjoyed in the days of the first

For teachers: You may want to invite class members or family members to participate in one or more of the following activities: (1) Read the additional scriptures listed at the end of the chapter, and discuss how the Holy Ghost helps us through our mortal journey. (2) Tell about some of the blessings that have come into their lives because they have the gift of the Holy Ghost. (3) Discuss what parents can do to help their children understand the gift of the Holy Ghost and how the Holy Ghost communicates with us.

Apostles. We believe in this gift in all its fulness, power, greatness, and glory. (See *Teachings of Presidents of the Church: Joseph Smith* [2007], 97–98.)

A person may be temporarily guided by the Holy Ghost without receiving the gift of the Holy Ghost (see D&C 130:23). However, this guidance will not be continuous unless the person is baptized and receives the laying on of hands for the gift of the Holy Ghost. We read in Acts 10 that the Roman soldier Cornelius received inspiration from the Holy Ghost so that he knew the gospel of Jesus Christ was true. But Cornelius did not receive the gift of the Holy Ghost until after he was baptized. The Prophet Joseph Smith taught that if Cornelius had not received baptism and the gift of the Holy Ghost, the Holy Ghost would have left him (see *Teachings of Presidents of the Church: Joseph Smith,* 97).

Today people who are not members of the Church learn by the power of the Holy Ghost that the Book of Mormon is true (see Moroni 10:4–5). But that initial testimony leaves them if they do not receive the gift of the Holy Ghost. They do not receive the continuing assurance that can come to those who have the gift of the Holy Ghost.

Receiving the Gift of the Holy Ghost

- What must we do to receive the constant companionship of the Holy Ghost?

After people are baptized, they are confirmed members of the Church and given the gift of the Holy Ghost by the laying on of hands. The Lord said, "Whoso having faith you shall confirm in my church, by the laying on of the hands, and I will bestow the gift of the Holy Ghost upon them" (D&C 33:15).

Every worthy elder of the Church, when authorized, may give the gift of the Holy Ghost to another person. However, there is no guarantee that the person will receive inspiration and guidance from the Holy Ghost just because the elders have laid their hands on his or her head. Each person must "receive the Holy Ghost." This means that the Holy Ghost will come to us only when we are faithful and desire help from this heavenly messenger.

To be worthy to have the help of the Holy Ghost, we must seek earnestly to obey the commandments of God. We must keep our thoughts and actions pure.

Recognizing the Influence of the Holy Ghost

The Holy Ghost usually communicates with us quietly. His influence is often referred to as a "still small voice" (see 1 Kings 19:9–12; Helaman 5:30; D&C 85:6). President Boyd K. Packer explained: "The Holy Ghost speaks with a voice that you *feel* more than you *hear*. . . . While we speak of 'listening' to the whisperings of the Spirit, most often one describes a spiritual prompting by saying, 'I had a feeling . . .'" He continued: "This voice of the Spirit speaks gently, prompting you what to do or what to say, or it may caution or warn you" (in Conference Report, Oct. 1994, 77; or *Ensign,* Nov. 1994, 60).

One of God's Greatest Gifts

- What blessings can we receive through the gift of the Holy Ghost?

The gift of the Holy Ghost is one of God's greatest gifts to us. Through the Holy Ghost we may know that God lives, that Jesus is the Christ, and that His Church has been restored to the earth. We may have the promptings of the Holy Ghost to show us all the things we should do (see 2 Nephi 32:5). The Holy Ghost sanctifies us to prepare us for God's presence. We may enjoy the gifts of the Spirit (see chapter 22 in this book). This great gift from our Heavenly Father can also bring peace to our hearts and an understanding of the things of God (see 1 Corinthians 2:9–12).

- Why is the gift of the Holy Ghost one of God's greatest gifts to us?

Additional Scriptures

- 1 Corinthians 3:16–17; D&C 130:22–23 (the Holy Ghost dwells with the faithful)
- Acts 19:1–7 (gift of the Holy Ghost bestowed anciently)

- Moroni 8:25–26 (how to receive the Holy Ghost)
- Moroni 10:5 (the Holy Ghost is a witness to truth)
- Mosiah 5:2 (the Holy Ghost changes hearts)
- Alma 5:54 (the Holy Ghost sanctifies)

The Gifts of the Spirit

Chapter 22

The Gifts of the Spirit

- What spiritual gifts does the Lord give us?

Following baptism, each of us had hands laid on our heads to receive the gift of the Holy Ghost. If we are faithful, we can have His influence continually with us. Through Him, each of us can be blessed with certain spiritual powers called gifts of the Spirit. These gifts are given to those who are faithful to Christ. "All these gifts come from God, for the benefit of the children of God" (D&C 46:26). They help us know and teach the truths of the gospel. They will help us bless others. They will guide us back to our Heavenly Father. To use our gifts wisely, we need to know what they are, how we can develop them, and how to recognize Satan's imitations of them.

The scriptures mention many gifts of the Spirit. These gifts have been given to members of the true Church whenever it has been on the earth (see Mark 16:16–18). The gifts of the Spirit include the following:

The Gift of Tongues (D&C 46:24)

Sometimes it is necessary to communicate the gospel in a language that is unfamiliar to us. When this happens, the Lord can bless us with the ability to speak that language. Many missionaries have received the gift of tongues (see the picture in this chapter). For example, Elder Alonzo A. Hinckley was a missionary in Holland who understood and spoke very little Dutch even though he had prayed and studied hard. When he returned to a home he had visited before,

---

For teachers: Consider asking each class member or family member to review the list of spiritual gifts in this chapter and choose two that they would like to learn more about. As part of the lesson, give them time on their own to study the paragraphs and scripture passages about the gifts they have chosen. When they have had time to study, ask them to share what they have learned.

몰몬경

a lady opened the door and spoke to him very angrily in Dutch. To his amazement he could understand every word. He felt a strong desire to bear his testimony to her in Dutch. He began to speak, and the words came out very clearly in Dutch. But when he returned to show his mission president that he could speak Dutch, the ability had left him. Many faithful members have been blessed with the gift of tongues. (See Joseph Fielding Smith, *Answers to Gospel Questions,* comp. Joseph Fielding Smith Jr., 5 vols. [1957–66], 2:32–33.)

The Gift of Interpretation of Tongues (D&C 46:25)

This gift is sometimes given to us when we do not understand a language and we need to receive an important message from God. For example, President David O. McKay had a great desire to speak to the Saints in New Zealand without an interpreter. He told them that he hoped that the Lord would bless them that they could understand him. He spoke in English. His message lasted about 40 minutes. As he spoke, he could tell by the expression on many of their faces and the tears in their eyes that they were receiving his message. (See *Answers to Gospel Questions,* 2:30–31.)

The Gift of Translation (D&C 5:4)

If we have been called by the leaders of the Church to translate the word of the Lord, we can receive a gift to translate beyond our natural ability. As with all gifts, we must live righteously, study hard, and pray to receive it. When we do these things, the Lord causes us to feel a burning inside concerning the correctness of the translation (see D&C 9:8–9). Joseph Smith had the gift of translation when he translated the Book of Mormon. This gift came to him only when he was in tune with the Spirit.

The Gift of Wisdom (D&C 46:17)

Some of us have been blessed with the ability to understand people and the principles of the gospel as they apply in our lives. We are told:

"If any of you lack wisdom, let him ask of God, that giveth to all men liberally, and upbraideth not; and it shall be given him.

Simon Dewey

commanded His people to partake of the sacrament in remembrance of Him, saying, "It is expedient that the church meet together often to partake of bread and wine in the remembrance of the Lord Jesus" (D&C 20:75).

How the Sacrament Is Administered

The scriptures explain exactly how the sacrament is to be administered. Members of the Church meet each Sabbath day to worship and partake of the sacrament (see D&C 20:75). The sacrament is administered by those who hold the necessary priesthood authority. A priest or Melchizedek Priesthood holder breaks bread into pieces, kneels, and blesses it (see D&C 20:76). A deacon or other priesthood holder then passes the sacrament bread to the congregation. Then the priest or Melchizedek Priesthood holder blesses the water, and it too is passed to the members. Jesus gave His disciples wine when He introduced the sacrament. However, in a latter-day revelation He has said that it doesn't matter what we eat and drink during the sacrament as long as we remember Him (see D&C 27:2–3). Today, Latter-day Saints drink water instead of wine.

Jesus has revealed the exact words for both sacrament prayers. We should listen carefully to these beautiful prayers and try to understand what we are promising and what is being promised to us. Here is the prayer that is offered to bless the bread:

"O God, the Eternal Father, we ask thee in the name of thy Son, Jesus Christ, to bless and sanctify this bread to the souls of all those who partake of it, that they may eat in remembrance of the body of thy Son, and witness unto thee, O God, the Eternal Father, that they are willing to take upon them the name of thy Son, and always remember him and keep his commandments which he has given them; that they may always have his Spirit to be with them. Amen" (D&C 20:77).

Here is the prayer that is offered to bless the water:

"O God, the Eternal Father, we ask thee in the name of thy Son, Jesus Christ, to bless and sanctify this wine [water] to the souls of all those who drink of it, that they may do it in remembrance of the blood of thy Son, which was shed for them; that they may witness unto thee,

O God, the Eternal Father, that they do always remember him, that they may have his Spirit to be with them. Amen" (D&C 20:79).

The ordinance of the sacrament is performed very simply and reverently.

- Carefully review the sacrament prayers. Think about the meaning of each phrase.

The Covenants We Renew during the Sacrament

- What covenants do we renew during the sacrament? What blessings does the Lord promise us as we keep those covenants?

Each time we partake of the sacrament, we renew covenants with the Lord. A covenant is a sacred promise between the Lord and His children. The covenants we make are clearly stated in the sacramental prayers. It is important to know what those covenants are and what they mean.

We covenant that we are willing to take upon ourselves the name of Jesus Christ. By this we show we are willing to be identified with Him and His Church. We commit to serve Him and our fellowman. We promise that we will not bring shame or reproach upon that name.

We covenant to always remember Jesus Christ. All our thoughts, feelings, and actions will be influenced by Him and His mission.

We promise to keep His commandments.

We take these obligations upon ourselves when we are baptized (see D&C 20:37; Mosiah 18:6–10). Thus, when we partake of the sacrament, we renew the covenants we made when we were baptized. Jesus gave us the pattern for partaking of the sacrament (see 3 Nephi 18:1–12) and said that when we follow this pattern, repenting of our sins and believing on His name, we will gain a remission of our sins (see Joseph Smith Translation, Matthew 26:24).

The Lord promises that if we keep our covenants, we will always have His Spirit to be with us. A person guided by the Spirit will have the knowledge, faith, power, and righteousness to gain eternal life.

- What can we do to remember these promises during the week?

Our Attitude When Partaking of the Sacrament

- How can we prepare ourselves to partake of the sacrament? What can we think about during the sacrament to help us remember the Savior's Atonement?

Before partaking of the sacrament, we are to prepare ourselves spiritually. The Lord emphasizes that no one should partake of the sacrament unworthily. That means we must repent of our sins before taking the sacrament. The scriptures say, "If any have trespassed, let him not partake until he makes reconciliation" (D&C 46:4). The Lord instructed His twelve Nephite disciples, "Ye shall not suffer any one knowingly to partake of my flesh and blood unworthily, when ye shall minister it; for whoso eateth and drinketh my flesh and blood unworthily eateth and drinketh damnation to his soul" (3 Nephi 18:28–29).

During the sacrament service we should dismiss from our minds all worldly thoughts. We should feel prayerful and reverent. We should think of the Atonement of our Savior and be grateful for it. We should examine our lives and look for ways to improve. We should also renew our determination to keep the commandments.

We do not need to be perfect before partaking of the sacrament, but we must have the spirit of repentance in our hearts. The attitude with which we partake of the sacrament influences our experience with it. If we partake of the sacrament with a pure heart, we receive the promised blessings of the Lord.

- Why do you think worthily partaking of the sacrament increases our spiritual strength?

Additional Scriptures

- 1 Corinthians 11:27–29 (partake of the sacrament worthily)
- John 4:5–14 (Jesus is the Living Water)
- John 6:30–35 (Jesus is the Bread of Life)

For teachers: If many of those you teach are parents, you may want to ask them to share ideas about how they can help their children prepare to partake of the sacrament reverently.

The Sabbath Day

Chapter 24

The Meaning of the Sabbath Day

• What is the Sabbath day?

"Remember the sabbath day, to keep it holy" (Exodus 20:8; see also D&C 68:29).

The word *Sabbath* comes from a Hebrew word meaning *rest.* Before the Resurrection of Jesus Christ, the Sabbath day commemorated God's day of rest after He finished the Creation. It was a sign of the covenant between God and His people. We read in the book of Genesis that God created the heavens and the earth in six periods of time, which He called days: "And on the seventh day God ended his work which he had made; and he rested on the seventh day from all his work which he had made. And God blessed the seventh day, and sanctified it" (Genesis 2:2–3). Now the Sabbath also commemorates the Resurrection of Jesus Christ.

The Sabbath day is every seventh day. It is a holy day ordained by God for us to rest from our daily labors and worship Him.

The Purpose of the Sabbath Day

• How would you explain the purpose of the Sabbath day to someone who does not know about the Sabbath?

Jesus taught that the Sabbath day was made for our benefit (see Mark 2:27). The purpose of the Sabbath is to give us a certain day of the week on which to direct our thoughts and actions toward God. It is not a day merely to rest from work. It is a sacred day to be spent in worship and reverence. As we rest from our usual daily activities, our minds are freed to ponder spiritual matters. On this day we should renew our covenants with the Lord and feed our souls on the things of the Spirit.

- Think about what you can do to keep the purpose of the Sabbath in mind as you prepare for the day each week.

History of the Sabbath

The seventh day was consecrated by God as a Sabbath in the beginning of the earth (see Genesis 2:2–3). Since earliest times, the tradition of a sacred seventh day has been preserved among various peoples of the earth. God renewed a commandment concerning this day to the Israelites, saying, "Remember the sabbath day, to keep it holy" (Exodus 20:8). Keeping the Sabbath day was also a sign that the Israelites were His covenant people (see Exodus 31:12–13, 16; Isaiah 56:1–8; Jeremiah 17:19–27).

However, some Jewish leaders made many unnecessary rules about the Sabbath. They decided how far people could walk, what kind of knots they could tie, and so forth. When certain Jewish leaders criticized Jesus Christ for healing sick people on the Sabbath, Jesus reminded them that the Sabbath was made for the benefit of man.

The Nephites also observed the Sabbath day according to the commandments of God (see Jarom 1:5).

In modern times the Lord has repeated His commandment that we should remember the Sabbath day and keep it holy (see D&C 68:29).

The Lord's Day

- Why was the Sabbath changed from the seventh day to the first day?

Until His Resurrection, Jesus Christ and His disciples honored the seventh day as the Sabbath. After His Resurrection, Sunday was held sacred as the Lord's day in remembrance of His Resurrection on that day (see Acts 20:7; 1 Corinthians 16:2). From that time on, His followers observed the first day of the week as their Sabbath. In both cases there were six days of labor and one for rest and devotion.

The Lord has given us a direct commandment in these days that we too should honor Sunday, the Lord's day, as our Sabbath (see D&C 59:12).

- How can the remembrance of the Resurrection influence our worship on the Sabbath?

Keeping the Sabbath Day Holy

- What does it mean to keep the Sabbath day holy?

The Lord asks us, first, to sanctify the Sabbath day. In a revelation given to Joseph Smith in 1831, the Lord commanded the Saints to go to the house of prayer and offer up their sacraments, rest from their labors, and pay their devotions to the Most High (see D&C 59:9–12).

Second, He asks us to rest from daily work. This means we should perform no labor that would keep us from giving our full attention to spiritual matters. The Lord told the Israelites, "Thou shalt not do any work, thou, nor thy son, nor thy daughter, thy manservant, nor thy maidservant, nor thy cattle" (Exodus 20:10). Our prophets have told us that we should not shop, hunt, fish, attend sports events, or participate in similar activities on that day.

President Spencer W. Kimball cautioned, however, that if we merely lounge about doing nothing on the Sabbath, we are not keeping the day holy. The Sabbath calls for constructive thoughts and acts. (See *Teachings of Presidents of the Church: Spencer W. Kimball* [2006], 170.)

What kinds of things *may* we do on the Sabbath? The prophet Isaiah suggested that we should turn away from doing our own pleasure and should "call the sabbath a delight, the holy of the Lord, honourable" (Isaiah 58:13).

We should consider righteous things we can do on the Sabbath. For example, we can keep the Sabbath day holy by attending Church meetings; reading the scriptures and the words of our Church leaders; visiting the sick, the aged, and our loved ones; listening to uplifting music and singing hymns; praying to our Heavenly Father with praise and thanksgiving; performing Church service; preparing family history records and personal histories; telling faith-promoting stories and bearing our testimony to family members and sharing

For teachers: You can help class members or family members think more deeply about a question by giving them time to ponder. After they have had enough time, ask for their responses.

spiritual experiences with them; writing letters to missionaries and loved ones; fasting with a purpose; and sharing time with children and others in the home.

In deciding what other activities we could properly engage in on the Sabbath, we could ask ourselves: Will it uplift and inspire me? Does it show respect for the Lord? Does it direct my thoughts to Him?

There may be times when we are required to work on the Sabbath. We should avoid this whenever possible, but when it is absolutely necessary, we should still maintain the spirit of Sabbath worship in our hearts as much as possible.

- Think about something you can do to improve in your efforts to keep the Sabbath day holy. If you are a parent or grandparent, think about something you can do to help your children or grandchildren understand the meaning of the Sabbath.

Blessings for Observing the Sabbath

- What are some blessings we receive when we keep the Sabbath day holy?

If we honor the Sabbath day, we may receive great spiritual and temporal blessings. The Lord has said that if we keep the Sabbath day with thanksgiving and cheerful hearts, we will be full of joy. He has promised:

"The fulness of the earth is yours, . . . whether for food or for raiment, or for houses, or for barns, or for orchards, or for gardens, or for vineyards;

"Yea, all things which come of the earth, in the season thereof, are made for the benefit and the use of man, both to please the eye and to gladden the heart;

"Yea, for food and for raiment, for taste and for smell, to strengthen the body and to enliven the soul" (D&C 59:16–19).

Additional Scriptures

- Exodus 31:16–17 (the Sabbath is a perpetual covenant between the Lord and His people)
- Mosiah 13:16–19; 18:23; Exodus 35:1–3; Leviticus 26:2–4, 6, 12 (observe the Sabbath as a holy day)
- Luke 6:1–11 (lawful to do good on the Sabbath)
- Luke 13:11–17; John 5:1–18 (Jesus's example of doing good on the Sabbath)

HOLY
BIBLE

Fasting

Chapter 25

How to Fast Properly

• What can we do to make fasting a joyful experience?

Since the time of Adam, God's people have fasted to help them draw near to Him and to worship Him. Jesus showed the importance of fasting by His own example (see Luke 4:1–4). Through latter-day revelation we learn that the Lord still expects His people to fast and pray often (see D&C 88:76).

Fasting means to go without food and drink. Occasional fasting is good for our bodies and helps our minds become more active.

The Savior taught us that purposeful fasting is more than just going without food and drink. We must also concentrate on spiritual matters.

We Should Pray When We Fast

Prayer is a necessary part of fasting. Throughout the scriptures, prayer and fasting are mentioned together. Our fasting should be accompanied by sincere prayer, and we should begin and end our fasting with prayer.

We Should Fast with a Purpose

Fasting can have many purposes. We can overcome weaknesses or problems by fasting and praying. Sometimes we may wish to fast and pray for help or guidance for others, such as a family member who is ill and needs a blessing (see Mosiah 27:22–23). Through fasting we can come to know the truth of things just as did the prophet Alma in the Book of Mormon. He said: "I have fasted and prayed

---

For teachers: You may want to divide class members or family members into groups of two to four people and give each group an opportunity to discuss ways to make fasting a joyful experience. Then work together to make a list of everyone's ideas—perhaps on the board or on a large piece of paper.

Christ's atoning sacrifice marked the end of sacrifices by the shedding of blood. Such outward sacrifice was replaced by the ordinance of the sacrament. The ordinance of the sacrament was given to remind us of the Savior's great sacrifice. We should partake of the sacrament often. The emblems of bread and water remind us of the Savior's body and of His blood, which He shed for us (see chapter 23 in this book).

- Why is the Atonement considered the great and last sacrifice?

We Still Must Sacrifice

- How do we observe the law of sacrifice today?

Even though sacrifice by the shedding of blood was ended, the Lord still asks us to sacrifice. But now He requires a different kind of offering. He said: "Ye shall offer up unto me no more the shedding of blood, . . . and your burnt offerings shall be done away. . . . And ye shall offer for a sacrifice unto me a broken heart and a contrite spirit" (3 Nephi 9:19–20). A "broken heart and a contrite spirit" means that we offer deep sorrow for our sins as we humble ourselves and repent of them.

We Must Be Willing to Sacrifice Everything We Have to the Lord

- Why are people willing to make sacrifices?

The Apostle Paul wrote that we should become living sacrifices, holy and acceptable unto God (see Romans 12:1).

If we are to be a living sacrifice, we must be willing to give everything we have for The Church of Jesus Christ of Latter-day Saints—to build the kingdom of God on the earth and labor to bring forth Zion (see 1 Nephi 13:37).

A rich young ruler asked the Savior, "What shall I do to inherit eternal life?" Jesus answered, "Thou knowest the commandments, Do not commit adultery, Do not kill, Do not steal, Do not bear false witness, Honour thy father and thy mother." And the rich man said, "All these have I kept from my youth." When Jesus heard this, He said, "Yet lackest thou one thing: sell all that thou hast, and distribute unto the poor, and thou shalt have treasure in heaven: and come, follow me." When the young man heard this, he was sorrowful. He was very rich and had his heart set on his riches. (See Luke 18:18–23; see also the picture in this chapter.)

The young ruler was a good man. But when he was put to the test, he was not willing to sacrifice his worldly possessions. On the other hand, the Lord's disciples Peter and Andrew were willing to sacrifice everything for the sake of the kingdom of God. When Jesus said unto them, "Follow me, . . . they straightway left their nets, and followed him" (Matthew 4:19–20).

Like the disciples, we can offer our daily activities as a sacrifice to the Lord. We can say, "Thy will be done." Abraham did this. He lived on the earth before Christ, in the days when sacrifices and burnt offerings were required. As a test of Abraham's faith, the Lord commanded him to offer up his son Isaac as a sacrifice. Isaac was the only son of Abraham and Sarah. The command to offer him as a sacrifice was extremely painful for Abraham.

Nevertheless, he and Isaac made the long journey to Mount Moriah, where the sacrifice was to be made. They traveled for three days. Imagine Abraham's thoughts and his heartache. His son was to be sacrificed to the Lord. When they reached Mount Moriah, Isaac carried the wood and Abraham carried the fire and the knife to the place where they were to build the altar. Isaac said, "My father . . . behold the fire and the wood: but where is the lamb for a burnt offering?" Abraham answered, "My son, God will provide himself a lamb." Then Abraham built an altar and arranged the wood on it. He bound Isaac and laid him upon the wood. He then took the knife to kill Isaac. At that moment an angel of the Lord stopped him, saying, "Abraham . . . lay not thine hand upon the lad, neither do thou any thing unto him: for now I know that thou fearest God, seeing thou hast not withheld thy son, thine only son from me." (See Genesis 22:1–14.)

Abraham must have been overcome with joy when he was no longer required to sacrifice his son. But he loved the Lord so much that he was willing to do anything the Lord asked.

- What examples of sacrifice have you observed in the lives of people you know? What examples of sacrifice have you seen in the lives of your ancestors? in the lives of early members of the Church? in the lives of people in the scriptures? What have you learned from these examples?

Sacrifice Helps Us Prepare to Live in the Presence of God

Only through sacrifice can we become worthy to live in the presence of God. Only through sacrifice can we enjoy eternal life. Many who have lived before us have sacrificed all they had. We must be willing to do the same if we would earn the rich reward they enjoy.

We may not be asked to sacrifice all things. But like Abraham, we should be willing to sacrifice everything to become worthy to live in the presence of the Lord.

The Lord's people have always sacrificed greatly and in many different ways. Some have suffered hardship and ridicule for the gospel. Some new converts to the Church have been cut off from their families. Lifetime friends have turned away. Some members have lost their jobs; some have lost their lives. But the Lord notices our sacrifices; He promises, "Every one that hath forsaken houses, or brethren, or sisters, or father, or mother, or wife, or children, or lands, for my name's sake, shall receive an hundredfold, and shall inherit everlasting life" (Matthew 19:29).

As our testimonies of the gospel grow, we become able to make greater sacrifices to the Lord. Note the sacrifices made in these true examples:

A member of the Church in Germany saved his tithing for years until someone with priesthood authority could come and accept it.

A Relief Society visiting teacher served for 30 years without missing an assignment.

A group of Saints in South Africa rode for three days, standing up, to be able to hear and see the prophet of the Lord.

At an area conference in Mexico, members of the Church slept on the ground and fasted during the days of the conference. They had used all their money just to get to the conference and had nothing left for food and shelter.

One family sold their car to get the money they wanted to contribute to a temple building fund.

Another family sold their home to get money to go to the temple.

Many faithful Latter-day Saints have very little to live on, yet they pay their tithes and offerings.

One brother sacrificed his job because he refused to work on Sunday.

In one branch, the youth gave freely and willingly of their time to care for the young children while their parents helped build the meetinghouse.

Young men and women give up or postpone good job opportunities, education, or sports to serve as missionaries.

Many more examples could be given of those who sacrifice for the Lord. Yet a place in our Heavenly Father's kingdom is worth any sacrifice we have to make of our time, talents, energy, money, and lives. Through sacrifice we can obtain a knowledge from the Lord that we are acceptable to Him (see D&C 97:8).

- Why do you think our willingness to sacrifice is related to our readiness to live in the presence of God?

Additional Scriptures

- Luke 12:16–34 (where the treasure is, there is the heart)
- Luke 9:57–62 (sacrifice to be fit for the kingdom)
- D&C 64:23; 97:12 (today is a day of sacrifice)
- D&C 98:13–15 (those who lose life for the Lord will find it)
- Alma 24 (the people of Ammon sacrifice their lives rather than break their oath to the Lord)

Work and Personal Responsibility

Chapter 27

Work Is an Eternal Principle

- What experiences have you had that have shown you the importance of work?

Our Heavenly Father and Jesus Christ have shown us by Their examples and teachings that work is important in heaven and on earth. God worked to create the heavens and the earth. He caused the seas to gather in one place and the dry land to appear. He caused grass, herbs, and trees to grow on the land. He created the sun, the moon, and the stars. He created every living thing in the sea or on the land. Then He placed Adam and Eve on the earth to take care of it and to have dominion over all living things. (See Genesis 1:1–28.)

Jesus said, "My Father worketh hitherto, and I work" (John 5:17). He also said, "I must work the works of him that sent me" (John 9:4).

We Are Commanded to Work

Work has been the way of life on earth since Adam and Eve left the Garden of Eden. The Lord said to Adam, "In the sweat of thy face shalt thou eat bread" (Genesis 3:19). Adam and Eve worked in the fields so they could provide for their own needs and the needs of their children (see Moses 5:1).

The Lord said to the people of Israel, "Six days shalt thou labour" (Exodus 20:9).

For teachers: Try to help each class member or family member participate during the lesson. Individuals may help by setting up chairs, offering the opening or closing prayer, writing on the board, reading scriptures aloud, answering questions, sharing testimony, or summarizing the lesson.

In the early days of the restored Church, the Lord told the Latter-day Saints, "Now, I, the Lord, am not well pleased with the inhabitants of Zion, for there are idlers among them" (D&C 68:31).

A prophet of God has said, "Work is to be reenthroned as the ruling principle of the lives of our Church membership" (Heber J. Grant, *Teachings of Presidents of the Church: Heber J. Grant* [2002], 115).

Family Responsibility

- What are some responsibilities that fathers, mothers, and children have to maintain a home? What can family members do to share in the work?

Parents work together to provide for the physical, spiritual, and emotional well-being of their family. They should never expect anyone to take care of this responsibility for them. The Apostle Paul wrote, "If any provide not for his own, and specially for those of his own house, he hath denied the faith" (1 Timothy 5:8).

Couples should seek inspiration from the Lord and follow the counsel of the prophets when establishing individual responsibilities. Creating a home where principles of the gospel are taught daily and where love and order abound is as important as providing the basic necessities of food and clothing.

Children should do their part in the work of the family. It is necessary for children to have work assignments to fit their abilities. They need to be praised for their successes. Good work attitudes, habits, and skills are learned through successful experiences in the home.

Sometimes people encounter hardships when trying to provide for their families. Chronic illness, the loss of a spouse, or the addition of an elderly parent can add to the responsibilities in a home. Our Heavenly Father remembers the families in these situations and gives them the strength to carry out their duties. He will always bless them if they ask Him in faith.

We Can Enjoy Our Work

- How does our attitude affect our work?

To some people work is a drudgery. To others it is an exciting part of life. One way to enjoy life's fullest benefits is to learn to love work.

Not all of us can choose the kind of work we do. Some of us labor for long hours for the bare necessities. It is difficult to enjoy such work. Yet the happiest people have learned to enjoy their work, whatever it is.

We can help one another in our work. The heaviest load becomes lighter when someone shares it.

Our attitude toward work is very important. The following story shows how one man saw beyond his daily labor. A traveler passed a stone quarry and saw three men working. He asked each man what he was doing. Each man's answer revealed a different attitude toward the same job. "I am cutting stone," the first man answered. The second replied, "I am earning three gold pieces per day." The third man smiled and said, "I am helping to build a house of God."

In any honest work we can serve God. King Benjamin, a Nephite prophet, said, "When ye are in the service of your fellow beings ye are only in the service of your God" (Mosiah 2:17). If our work provides only enough for necessities for ourselves or our families, we are still helping some of God's children.

- How can we improve our attitude about work?

God Condemns Idleness

The Lord is not pleased with those who are lazy or idle. He said, "The idler shall not have place in the church, except he repent and mend his ways" (D&C 75:29). He also commanded, "Thou shalt not be idle; for he that is idle shall not eat the bread nor wear the garments of the laborer" (D&C 42:42).

From the earliest days of the Church, the prophets have taught Latter-day Saints to be independent and self-sustaining and to avoid idleness. True Latter-day Saints will not voluntarily shift from themselves the burden of their own support. So long as they are able, they will supply themselves and their families with the necessities of life.

As far as they are able, all Church members should accept the responsibility to care for their relatives who are unable to provide for themselves.

- How does idleness affect an individual? a family? a community?

Work, Recreation, and Rest

- Why is it important to keep a balance in life between work, recreation, and rest?

We should each find the proper balance between work, recreation, and rest. There is an old saying: "Doing nothing is the hardest work of all, because one can never stop to rest." Without work, rest and relaxation have no meaning.

Not only is it pleasant and necessary to rest, but we are commanded to rest on the Sabbath day (see Exodus 20:10; D&C 59:9–12). This day of rest after each six days of labor brings refreshment for the days that follow. The Lord also promises the "fulness of the earth" to those who observe the Sabbath day (see D&C 59:16–20; see also chapter 24 in this book).

On other days of the week, in addition to working, we may spend time to improve our talents and enjoy our hobbies, recreation, or other activities that will refresh us.

- What can we do to keep a good balance between work, recreation, and rest? How can parents help their children maintain this balance?

The Blessings of Work

- What are some blessings that come from honest work?

God revealed to Adam, "In the sweat of thy face shalt thou eat bread" (Genesis 3:19). In addition to being a temporal law, this was a law for the salvation of Adam's soul. There is no real division between spiritual, mental, and physical work. Work is essential to each of us for growth, character development, and many satisfactions that the idle never know.

a note that read, "If you want anyone to do errands, call us." The widow was gladdened by the small kindness and never forgot it.

Sometimes, however, we must sacrifice greatly to serve someone. The Savior gave up His life in serving us.

- Think about people in your family or community who are in need economically, socially, physically, or spiritually. Ponder things you can do to serve them.

Why the Savior Wants Us to Serve Others

- Why does the Lord want us to serve others?

Through the service of men and women and boys and girls, God's work is done. President Spencer W. Kimball explained: "God does notice us, and he watches over us. But it is usually through another person that he meets our needs" (*Teachings of Presidents of the Church: Spencer W. Kimball* [2006], 82).

Throughout our lives all of us depend on others for help. When we were infants, our parents fed, clothed, and cared for us. Without this care we would have died. When we grew up, other people taught us skills and attitudes. Many of us have needed nursing care during illness or money in a financial crisis. Some of us ask God to bless suffering people and then do nothing for them. We must remember that God works through us.

When we help one another, we serve God. King Benjamin, a great king in Book of Mormon times, taught his people this principle by the way he lived. He served them all his life, earning his own living instead of being supported by the people. In an inspired sermon he explained why he loved service, saying:

"When ye are in the service of your fellow beings ye are only in the service of your God. . . .

"And if I, whom ye call your king, do labor to serve you, then ought not ye to labor to serve one another?" (Mosiah 2:17–18).

- What can we do to be ready to meet the needs of others?

We Receive Blessings through Service

• What blessings do we receive through service to others?

When we serve others we gain important blessings. Through service we increase our ability to love. We become less selfish. As we think of the problems of others, our own problems seem less serious. We must serve others to gain eternal life. God has said that those who live with Him must love and serve His children (see Matthew 25:34–40).

When we consider the lives of people who serve unselfishly, we can see that they gain more than they give. One such person was a Latter-day Saint named Paul who lost the use of both legs in an accident. Some men might have become bitter and useless, but Paul chose to think of others instead. He learned a trade and earned enough money to buy a house. There he and his wife made room for many homeless, unwanted children. Some were badly handicapped. Until his death 20 years later, he served these children and others. In return he was greatly loved, and his thoughts turned away from his crippled legs. He grew close to the Lord.

President Spencer W. Kimball said, "We become more substantive as we serve others—indeed, it is easier to 'find' ourselves because there is so much more of us to find!" (*Teachings of Presidents of the Church: Spencer W. Kimball,* 85–86).

Opportunities to Serve

Some of us serve only those we enjoy being around and avoid all others. However, Jesus commanded us to love and serve everyone. There are many opportunities to serve (see Mosiah 4:15–19).

We can serve members of our families. Husbands and wives should be aware of each other's needs. Parents should serve their children not only by feeding and clothing them but also by teaching and by playing and working with them. Children can serve by helping with household chores and by helping brothers and sisters.

Husbands and wives serve and help each other. They can help each other take care of the children, and they can support one another in their individual interests and pursuits. A mother and father may sacrifice to send a child on a mission. An older boy may comfort a little sister who is afraid of the dark or help her learn to read. Our prophets have told us that a family is the most important unit in society. We must serve our families well (see Mosiah 4:14–15).

We have many opportunities to serve our neighbors, our friends, and even strangers. If a neighbor is having difficulty harvesting crops before a storm, we can help. If a mother is ill, we can watch her children or help with the housework. If a young man is falling away from the Church, we can lead him back. If a child is ridiculed, we can befriend him and persuade others to be kind. We do not need to know the people we serve. We should look for ways to serve as many of our Heavenly Father's children as we can.

If we have special talents, we should use them to serve others. God blesses us with talents and abilities to help improve the lives of others.

We have opportunities to serve in the Church. One purpose of the Church organization is to give us opportunities to help each other. Members of the Church serve by doing missionary work, accepting leadership assignments, visiting other Church members, teaching classes, and doing other Church work. In The Church of Jesus Christ of Latter-day Saints there is no professional clergy, so the lay members must carry on all of the activities of the Church.

- How can we give enough time to our family, even with our many opportunities to give service in the Church and community?

Jesus Christ Is the Perfect Example of Service

- What are some of your favorite scripture stories in which the Savior sets an example of service?

The Savior provided the perfect example of service. He explained that He didn't come to earth to be served but to serve and to give His life for us (see Matthew 20:28).

For teachers: When we share our testimonies of Jesus Christ, we invite the influence of the Holy Ghost. As you prepare and teach, frequently look for ways to testify of the Savior and to invite those you teach to do the same.

Jesus Christ loves all of us more than we can understand. When He was on earth He served the poor, the ignorant, the sinner, the despised. He taught the gospel to all who would listen, fed crowds of hungry people who came to hear Him, healed the sick, and raised the dead.

He is the Creator of the earth and our Savior, yet He did many humble acts of service. Just before His Crucifixion He met with His disciples. After teaching them, He took a basin of water and a towel and washed their feet (see John 13:4–10; see also the picture in this chapter). In those days washing a visitor's feet was a sign of honor and was usually done by a servant. Jesus did it as an example of love and service. When we willingly serve others in the spirit of love, we become more like Christ.

- What can we learn from the Savior's example of service?

Additional Scriptures

- Mosiah 2 (King Benjamin's discourse on service)
- D&C 81:5 (succor, lift, strengthen)
- Colossians 3:23–24 (serve others as you would serve the Lord)
- Alma 17–18 (Ammon served the king)
- Galatians 5:13 (serve one another by love)

The Lord's Law of Health

Chapter 29

Our Bodies Are Temples of God

One of the great blessings we received when we came to earth was a physical body. We need a physical body to become like our Heavenly Father. Our bodies are so important that the Lord calls them temples of God (see 1 Corinthians 3:16–17; 6:19–20). Our bodies are holy.

Because our bodies are important, our Father in Heaven wants us to take good care of them. He knows that we can be happier, better people if we are healthy. The Holy Ghost can be with us if our bodies and minds are clean. Our Father knows that we face temptations to treat our bodies unwisely or to take harmful things into them. For this reason He has told us which things are good for our health and which things are bad. Much of the information God has given us concerning good health is found in Doctrine and Covenants 89. This revelation is called the Word of Wisdom.

We must obey the Word of Wisdom to be worthy to enter the temple. If we do not obey the Word of Wisdom, the Lord's Spirit withdraws from us. If we defile the "temple of God," which is our body, we hurt ourselves physically and spiritually.

We Are Commanded Not to Take Certain Things into Our Bodies

• What has the Lord commanded us not to take into our bodies?

The Lord commands us not to use wine and strong drinks, meaning drinks containing alcohol. The First Presidency has taught that strong drink often brings cruelty, poverty, disease, and plague into

the home. It often is a cause of dishonesty, loss of chastity, and loss of good judgment. It is a curse to all who drink it. (See "Message of the First Presidency," *Improvement Era,* Nov. 1942, 686.) Expectant mothers who drink can cause physical and mental damage to their children. Many automobile accidents are caused each year by people who drink alcohol.

The Lord has also told us that "tobacco is not for the body" (D&C 89:8). It is harmful to our bodies and our spirits. We should not smoke cigarettes or cigars or use chewing tobacco. Scientists have shown that tobacco causes many diseases and can harm unborn children.

The Lord also counsels us against the use of "hot drinks" (D&C 89:9). Church leaders have said that this means coffee and tea, which contain harmful substances. We should avoid all drinks that contain harmful substances.

We should not use drugs except when they are necessary as medicine. Some drugs are even more harmful than alcohol and tobacco (which are also drugs). Those who misuse drugs need to seek help, pray for strength, and counsel with their bishop so they can fully repent and become clean.

We should avoid anything that we know is harmful to our bodies. We should not use any substance that is habit forming. We should also avoid overeating. The Word of Wisdom does not tell us everything to avoid or consume, but it does give us guidelines. It is a valuable temporal law. It is also a great spiritual law. By living the Word of Wisdom, we become stronger spiritually. We purify our bodies so the Spirit of the Lord can dwell with us.

- What are some things that are not specifically mentioned in the Word of Wisdom that we should avoid?

For teachers: Writing lists can generate interest and help learners focus their attention. As class members or family members discuss substances that the Lord has commanded us not to take into our bodies, you may want to ask someone to write their answers on the board or on a large piece of paper. You could do the same when they discuss things that are healthful for our bodies.

We Are Taught That Certain Things Are Good for Our Bodies

- According to the Word of Wisdom, what are some things the Lord says are good for us?

Fruits, vegetables, and wholesome herbs are good for us. We should use them with wisdom and thanksgiving.

The flesh of birds and animals is also provided for our food. However, we should eat meat sparingly (see D&C 49:18; 89:12). Fish is also good for us to eat.

Grains are good for us. Wheat is especially good for us.

- How has the use of these things blessed you?

Work, Rest, and Exercise Are Important

- What do work, rest, and exercise have to do with the Lord's law of health?

In addition to Doctrine and Covenants 89, other scriptures tell us how to be healthy. They tell us that we should "cease to be idle; cease to be unclean; . . . cease to sleep longer than is needful; retire to thy bed early, that ye may not be weary; arise early, that your bodies and your minds may be invigorated" (D&C 88:124). We are also told, "Six days shalt thou labour, and do all thy work" (Exodus 20:9). The Lord counsels us not to labor more than we have strength for (see D&C 10:4).

A latter-day prophet has told us that we should keep our bodies healthy. He counseled, "Nutritious meals, regular exercise, and appropriate sleep are necessary for a strong body, just as consistent scripture study and prayer strengthen the mind and spirit" (Thomas S. Monson, in Conference Report, Oct. 1990, 60; or *Ensign,* Nov. 1990, 46).

Promised Blessings for Living the Lord's Law of Health

- What blessings come to us as we obey the Word of Wisdom?

Our Heavenly Father has given us health laws to teach us how to care for our bodies. The scriptures tell us about God's laws:

"No temporal commandment gave I . . . , for my commandments are spiritual" (D&C 29:35). This means that His commandments concerning our physical state are for our spiritual good.

When we keep the Lord's law of health and obey His other commandments, the Lord promises to bless us physically and spiritually.

Physically we have been promised good health. As a result of this good health we "shall run and not be weary, and shall walk and not faint" (D&C 89:20). This is a great blessing, but the spiritual blessings He has promised us are even greater than the physical ones.

The Lord promises us that we "shall find wisdom and great treasures of knowledge, even hidden treasures" (D&C 89:19). We will be taught important truths by the Holy Ghost through revelation. President Boyd K. Packer taught: "Our physical body is the instrument of our spirit. In that marvelous revelation the Word of Wisdom, we are told how to keep our bodies free from impurities which might dull, even destroy, those delicate physical senses which have to do with spiritual communication. The Word of Wisdom is a key to individual revelation" (in Conference Report, Oct. 1989, 16; or *Ensign,* Nov. 1989, 14).

The Lord also promises that the destroying angel shall pass us by. President Heber J. Grant said, "If you and I desire the blessings of life, of health, of vigor of body and mind; if we desire the destroying angel to pass us by, as he did in the days of the children of Israel, we must obey the Word of Wisdom; then God is bound, and the blessing shall come to us" (*Teachings of Presidents of the Church: Heber J. Grant* [2002], 192).

- How can we help children and youth understand the eternal significance of the Word of Wisdom?
- What can we do to help family members or friends who have difficulty obeying the Word of Wisdom?

Additional Scriptures

- Judges 13:13–14; Proverbs 20:1; Isaiah 5:11–12; Daniel 1 (avoid strong drink)
- D&C 59:16–20 (things of the earth for the benefit of man)

- Proverbs 23:20–21 (warning against drunkenness, gluttony, laziness)
- D&C 136:24 (cease drunkenness)

Charity

Chapter 30

What Is Charity?

• How would you define charity?

The life of the Savior reflects His pure love for all people. He even gave His life for us. Charity is that pure love which our Savior Jesus Christ has. He has commanded us to love one another as He loves us. The scriptures tell us that charity comes from a pure heart (see 1 Timothy 1:5). We have pure love when, from the heart, we show genuine concern and compassion for all our brothers and sisters.

Charity Is the Greatest of All Virtues

The prophet Mormon tells us, "Wherefore, cleave unto charity, which is the greatest of all, for all things must fail—but charity is the pure love of Christ, and it endureth forever" (Moroni 7:46–47; see also 1 Corinthians 13; 2 Nephi 26:30; Moroni 7:44–45, 48).

The Savior gave us the example of His life to follow. He was the Son of God. He had perfect love, and He showed us how to love. By His example, He showed us that the spiritual and physical needs of our fellowmen are as important as our own. Before He gave His life for us, He said:

"This is my commandment, That ye love one another, as I have loved you.

"Greater love hath no man than this, that a man lay down his life for his friends" (John 15:12–13).

Speaking to the Lord, Moroni said:

"I remember that thou hast said that thou hast loved the world, even unto the laying down of thy life for the world. . . .

"And now I know that this love which thou hast had for the children of men is charity; wherefore, except men shall have charity they cannot inherit that place which thou hast prepared in the mansions of thy Father" (Ether 12:33–34).

It may not be necessary for us to give our lives as the Savior did. But we can have charity if we make Him the center of our lives and follow His example and teachings. Like the Savior, we too can bless the lives of our brothers and sisters here on earth.

- Why is charity the greatest of all virtues?

Charity Includes Giving to the Sick, Afflicted, and Poor

The Savior gave us many teachings in the form of stories or parables. The parable of the good Samaritan teaches us that we should give to those in need, regardless of whether they are our friends or not (see Luke 10:30–37; see also James E. Talmage, *Jesus the Christ,* 3rd ed. [1916], 430–32). In the parable, the Savior said that a man was traveling to another city. On the road he was attacked by bandits. They stole his clothes and money and beat him, leaving him half dead. A priest came along, saw him, and passed him by. Then a temple attendant walked over, looked at him, and went on. However, a Samaritan, who was despised by the Jews, came along, and when he saw the man he felt compassion (see the picture in this chapter). Kneeling beside him, the good Samaritan bandaged his wounds and took him on a donkey to an inn. He paid the innkeeper to take care of the man until he recovered.

Jesus taught that we should give food to the hungry, shelter to those who have none, and clothes to the poor. When we visit the sick and those who are in prison, it is as if we were doing these things for Him instead. He promises that as we do these things, we will inherit His kingdom. (See Matthew 25:34–46.)

We should not try to decide whether someone really deserves our help or not (see Mosiah 4:16–24). If we have taken care of our own family's needs first, then we should help all who need help. In this way we will be like our Father in Heaven, who causes rain to fall on the just and on the unjust alike (see Matthew 5:44–45).

President Thomas S. Monson reminded us that there are those who need more than material goods:

"Let us ask ourselves the questions: 'Have I done any good in the world today? Have I helped anyone in need?' [*Hymns,* no. 223]. What a formula for happiness! What a prescription for contentment, for inner peace—to have inspired gratitude in another human being.

"Our opportunities to give of ourselves are indeed limitless, but they are also perishable. There are hearts to gladden. There are kind words to say. There are gifts to be given. There are deeds to be done. There are souls to be saved" (in Conference Report, Oct. 2001, 72; or *Ensign,* Nov. 2001, 60).

- In the parable of the good Samaritan, how would you describe those who passed the injured man? How would you describe the Samaritan? In what ways can we apply the message of this parable in our lives?

Charity Comes from the Heart

- How can we love people in spite of their sins and faults?

Even when we give to those in need, unless we feel compassion for them we do not have charity (see 1 John 3:16–17). The Apostle Paul taught that when we have charity we are filled with good feelings for all people. We are patient and kind. We are not boastful or proud, selfish or rude. When we have charity we do not remember or rejoice in the evil others have done. Neither do we do good things just because it is to our advantage. Instead, we share the joy of those who live by truth. When we have charity we are loyal, we believe the best of others, and we are kind to them. The scriptures teach that "charity never faileth." (See 1 Corinthians 13:4–8.)

The Savior was our example of how to feel toward and treat others. He despised wickedness, but He loved sinners in spite of their sins. He had compassion for children, the elderly, the poor, and the needy. He had such great love that He could beg our Heavenly Father to forgive the soldiers who drove the nails into His hands and feet (see Luke 23:34). He taught us that if we do not forgive others, our Father in Heaven will not forgive us (see Matthew 18:33–35).

He said: "I say unto you, Love your enemies, bless them that curse you, do good to them that hate you, and pray for them which despitefully use you, and persecute you. . . . For if ye love them which love you, what reward have ye?" (Matthew 5:44, 46). We must learn to feel toward others as Jesus did.

Developing the Virtue of Charity

- How can we become more charitable?

One way we can become charitable is by studying the life of Jesus Christ and keeping His commandments. We can study what He did in certain situations and do the same things when we are in the same kinds of situations.

Second, when we have uncharitable feelings, we can pray to have greater charity. Mormon urges us, "Pray unto the Father with all the energy of heart, that ye may be filled with this love [charity], which he hath bestowed upon all who are true followers of his Son, Jesus Christ" (Moroni 7:48).

Third, we can learn to love ourselves, which means that we understand our true worth as children of our Heavenly Father. The Savior taught that we must love others *as we love ourselves* (see Matthew 22:39). To love ourselves, we must respect and trust ourselves. This means that we must be obedient to the principles of the gospel. We must repent of any wrongdoings. We must forgive ourselves when we have repented. We will come to love ourselves better when we can feel the deep, comforting assurance that the Savior truly loves us.

Fourth, we can avoid thinking we are better than other people. We can have patience with their faults. Joseph Smith said, "The nearer we get to our heavenly Father, the more we are disposed to look with compassion on perishing souls; we feel that we want to take

---

For teachers: Under the heading "Developing the Virtue of Charity," each of the first four paragraphs teaches one way we can become more charitable. If the setting allows for small group discussion, consider dividing class members or family members into groups of four. Assign one of the four paragraphs to each member of each group. Invite participants to study their assigned paragraphs individually. Ask them to think of examples, from the lives of people they know or people in the scriptures, that represent this way of becoming charitable. Then ask them to share their examples with each other in their groups.

them upon our shoulders, and cast their sins behind our backs" (*Teachings of Presidents of the Church: Joseph Smith* [2007], 428–29).

In the Book of Mormon we read of Enos, a young man who wanted to know that his sins had been forgiven. He tells us:

"My soul hungered; and I kneeled down before my Maker, and I cried unto him in mighty prayer and supplication for mine own soul; and all the day long did I cry unto him; yea, and when the night came I did still raise my voice high that it reached the heavens.

"And there came a voice unto me, saying: Enos, thy sins are forgiven thee, and thou shalt be blessed" (Enos 1:4–5).

The Lord explained to Enos that because of his faith in Christ his sins had been forgiven. When Enos heard these words he no longer was concerned about himself. He knew the Lord loved him and would bless him. He began instead to feel concern for the welfare of his friends and relatives, the Nephites. He poured out his whole soul unto God for them. The Lord answered and said they would be blessed according to their faithfulness in keeping the commandments they had already been given. Enos's love increased even further after these words, and he prayed with many long strugglings for the Lamanites, who were the enemies of the Nephites. The Lord granted his desires, and he spent the rest of his life trying to save the souls of the Nephites and the Lamanites. (See Enos 1:6–26.)

Enos was so grateful for the Lord's love and forgiveness that he willingly spent the rest of his life helping others receive this same gift. Enos had become truly charitable. We too can do so. In fact, we must do so to inherit the place that has been prepared for us in our Father's kingdom.

Additional Scriptures

- Colossians 3:12–14 (charity is the bond of perfectness)
- Alma 34:28–29 (our prayers are vain if we do not act charitably)
- 1 Corinthians 12:29–13:3 (definition of charity)
- D&C 121:45–46 (let us be full of charity toward all people)

Honesty

Chapter 31

Honesty Is a Principle of Salvation

• What would society be like if everyone were perfectly honest?

The 13th article of faith says, "We believe in being honest." The Book of Mormon tells us about a group of people who were "distinguished for their zeal towards God, and also towards men; for they were perfectly honest and upright in all things; and they were firm in the faith of Christ, even unto the end" (Alma 27:27). Because of their honesty, these people were noted by their fellowmen and by God. It is important to learn what honesty is, how we are tempted to be dishonest, and how we can overcome this temptation.

Complete honesty is necessary for our salvation. President Brigham Young said, "If we accept salvation on the terms it is offered to us, we have got to be honest in every thought, in our reflections, in our meditations, in our private circles, in our deals, in our declarations, and in every act of our lives" (*Teachings of Presidents of the Church: Brigham Young* [1997], 293).

God is honest and just in all things (see Alma 7:20). We too must be honest in all things to become like Him. The brother of Jared testified, "Yea, Lord, I know that thou . . . art a God of truth, and canst not lie" (Ether 3:12). In contrast, the devil is a liar. In fact, he is the father of lies (see 2 Nephi 9:9). "Those who choose to cheat and lie and deceive and misrepresent become his slaves" (Mark E. Petersen, in Conference Report, Oct. 1971, 65; or *Ensign,* Dec. 1971, 73).

Honest people love truth and justice. They are honest in their words and actions. They do not lie, steal, or cheat.